ENCOUNTERS
---WITH---
WISDOM

ENCOUNTERS ---WITH--- WISDOM

BOOK FOUR

Thomas Hora, M. D.

The PAGL Foundation
Old Lyme, CT

Published by the PAGL Foundation
P.O. Box 4001, Old Lyme, CT 06371

Library of Congress Cataloging-in-Publication Data

ISBN 13: 978-0913105221

ISBN 10: 0-91310522-8

LCCN: 0913105015

Contents

Editors' Preface

This book presents dialogues between Dr. Thomas Hora, psychiatrist, spiritual teacher, and founder of Existential Metapsychiatry, and some of his students. They occurred in the late 1980s through 1995. Dr. Hora recorded most of the group sessions with his students and made the recordings available to those who attended. The PAGL Foundation[1] has collected many of these tapes and transcribed them. For the reader new to the teachings of Metapsychiatry, it is suggested that these dialogues will be more meaningful if one of Dr. Hora's other books, especially *Beyond the Dream,* is read first.

Dr. Hora maintained his practice in his homes (an apartment in New York City and a house in Bedford, New York). Group sessions were held in the living room, where chairs were arranged in a circle. After the students had gathered, Dr. Hora would enter and sit down. He greeted each student nonverbally, with eye contact and a smile, and then he waited for a question to be asked. If no question was forthcoming, Dr. Hora opened the dialogue.

Metapsychiatry values the sincere question, and Dr. Hora always waited for students to formulate questions. He listened for sincerity, as this indicated a student's receptivity and desire to understand. Sometimes a question might be phrased in an awkward or convoluted way; in such instances, some of the meandering has been edited here for the sake of clarity.

---

[1] PAGL is an acronym for Peace, Assurance, Gratitude, and Love, qualities of consciousness that are the fruit of spiritual progress. The PAGL Foundation was established to make Dr. Hora's work available (see *www.pagl.org*).

As a dialogue progressed, there could be long silences or pauses. At such times, Dr. Hora might introduce an entirely new topic, perhaps discerning an unasked question. He saw and was amused by the paradoxes that life offered, as he often demonstrated through asides and humorous remarks. He showed his students how to laugh at their woes by lifting their vision to a higher perspective, helping them make the distinction between taking something seriously and giving it full attention. Laughter erupted frequently.

Overall, the editors have chosen to keep the flow of the dialogue as it occurred, so no major changes have been made other than to maintain the anonymity of the participants and improve readability. Occasionally, Dr. Hora paraphrased or rephrased quotations from Scripture to emphasize a point. Where this occurs, a footnote has been provided with the original scriptural quotation and reference for clarification. Although some of the ideas in these dialogues may have been addressed in various ways in other available materials, to the sincere student, the freshness of these sessions can offer new insights and reinforce old ones.

* * *

December 5, 2015

1

Listen, Hear, Respond

Student: Two weeks ago, you were talking about leaving bad situations. You described a hospital you had left. I was trying to follow that. I think you may have answered the question, but I didn't understand it. When to leave and when not to leave, given that scenario described vs. the story of Daniel, who also was in a malevolent situation but stayed. What's the difference? I mean, it's not only for a job situation, but any idea that comes your way, whether to accept it or reject it and how to work with it. Could you explain what the difference is?

Dr. Hora: What hospital are you referring to?

Student: You referred to some situation where people were dying and you elected to leave, or something like that.

Dr. Hora: Well, God lets you know what is the right thing to do, if you listen.

Student: So the decision is made for you.

Dr. Hora: Right. Of course. We don't make decisions. Didn't you know that? (*Laughter*) We are guided, governed, inspired...and we respond. You would like to have a standard procedure so you would always know what to do in every situation?

10

Student: Not so much that as opposed to where the difference is. Could Daniel have elected to leave and not be a beneficial presence?

Dr. Hora: Well, Daniel was totally under Divine control. He was praying all day and all night and listening to what God had to say. He had a mission from God to reveal to people the reality of God. So he did his best under the circumstances. Jesus tried to escape the Crucifixion. Did you know that? You didn't know that? How come you didn't know that?

Student: I didn't know that.

Dr. Hora: He said to God, "Father, if it be possible, let this cup pass me by." But there was no answer, and he understood that he had to go through this ordeal of crucifixion. I think that's what the Bible says. I wasn't there, you know. (*Laughter*) Don't hold me to it. I am only telling you what I read in the Bible, and it has a meaning, of course. But all enlightenment and everything we are studying here is designed to help us to learn to listen, to hear, and to respond. That's the whole of Metapsychiatry and the essence of enlightenment: to listen, to hear. As the Bible says, "He that hath an ear, let him hear" (Revelation 2:7, 11, 17, 29), and we respond. We respond to the call and the inspired wisdom that is forever communicating to us. Most of us don't really listen (*laughing*).

Student: In attempting to listen, even though I would always like to, whenever there is choice, I would like to hear God say, "Turn right rather than left," and I have never heard that. It seems to me in my life that somehow circumstances come about by surprise rather than by choice, or the right choices, and I would rather have the right choices than somehow practice patience for circumstances to ultimately come about that are peaceful or comfortable or nice or whatever. Is there such a way that we can listen and somehow be led to a right choice?

Dr. Hora: Well, if you listen, you don't have to choose. You hear the message...but most people will tell you the trouble is that God isn't listening (*laughing*). I know somebody who was complaining, "I pray and I pray, and He doesn't do anything!"

Student: What seems like intuition or "sixth sense" or instinct is really God speaking to us?

Dr. Hora: You have to be radically sincere; otherwise, you will fool yourself. If you haven't learned yet to be completely sincere at every moment of your life, then whom can you trust?

Student: When I look back, there were times I just went to the right, and I thought I didn't know why, but it turned out to be the right move. I realize now that it was God telling me which way to go. But I didn't know that then. So somehow, sometimes it just seems like the right way to go.

Dr. Hora: And we go, and it's OK.

Student: And it's OK.

Dr. Hora: Thank God for that.

Student: Thank God, yes.

Student: Does that mean we are hearing Divine ideas? I mean, it's spontaneous that we seem to be moving.

Dr. Hora: And how can we know? It's very simple. If we have an idea about some movement or action or choice, and if we are at peace with it, that's a pretty good bet that it has God's approval and it is God's idea. But if we are deceiving ourselves, there is anxiety, because we are lying. That is very frequently the case. So we are taught to be very sincere under all circumstances. Most people who agonize over decisions and complain about things not working right and facing troubles usually are not listening. They want God to listen, which stands to reason. It would be nice if we could have a handle on God, right? It would be wonderful...but then He would get a big head.

When our prayers seem to be futile and frustrated and God seems to be unavailable, it is usually that we want something to be the way we want it. We have a tendency to be very operational, and then we say, "Well, I prayed, didn't I?"

Student: Is it possible, Dr. Hora, to be humble without being enlightened?

Dr. Hora: Sure, sure. Humility is just a prerequisite for the coming of enlightenment. You see, when you are enlightened, you don't have to be humble anymore. Humility is a tricky thing, because you can put it on. You can pretend.

Student: I am not sure I actually understand exactly what it is.

Dr. Hora: Most people think that humility is a form of behavior. All the pious people, the saints and the learned people, we watch them, how they behave, what their attitude is, and if we are interested in humility, we try to emulate them. But that is not humility; that is just a put-on. It seems like it's a quality that can be done. If something can be done, it is not of God. Isn't that interesting?

Student: I guess things that are done are in the sight of others...I mean, you can do something in the sight of people, but you can't *do* anything in the sight of God.

Dr. Hora: Well, you could do something in the sight of God if God told you to go ahead and do it (*laughing*).

Student: What is humility, true humility?

Dr. Hora: True humility: Jesus defined it in very simple terms. "Of mine own self I can do nothing...it is the Father who dwelleth in me, He doeth the works" (John 5:30, 14:10). This is humility. This is a beautiful, simple clarification of a concept. You cannot pretend humility. That's a lie. Many good, religious people work hard on expressing humility, and they wind up with a form of behavior that turns out to be hypocrisy. And many sincere people turn away from God because they don't want to be hypocrites. You see, that's the problem. Only radical sincerity will protect you from being a hypocrite and behaving as if you were humble.

Student: So if we are radically sincere, we are aware of our motivation at all times and of our thoughts, no matter how unpleasant they may seem to be?

Dr. Hora: Yes. Awareness of motivation is very important.

Student: So, Dr. Hora, in line with what you said before, if we listen, and we hear and we respond to the idea, then that results in doing something, generally.

Dr. Hora: No, it's not a doing; it's a responding.

Student: It's a responding. But it seems like a doing, even though the motivation could be right. I don't understand. How is there a difference between responding and doing?

Dr. Hora: When we are responding, we are not *doing* the responding. God impels us to go here or to go there. It is like compassion. People frequently try to put on compassion. The idea is that you can behave in a compassionate way. Again, that is self-deception. Compassion is God's doing in consciousness. It is happening in consciousness, and similarly humility. Whatsoever God doeth, says the Bible, is forever, and it is perfect. Nothing can be put into it or taken away from it. It is just the right response, which is impelled by the Divine Mind. God is this Mind, and He can impel certain turning here and turning there. There is this saying in the Bible: "You will hear a voice behind you, saying, 'This is the way;

walk ye in it' when you turn to the right or you turn to the left" (Isaiah 30:21). Here is a presentation of what is meant by Divine guidance. The ego has nothing to do with it. It is consciousness responding to a higher intelligence, and the result is harmonious, effortless, efficient, effective, and pretty good. (*Laughter*) And sometimes we are amazed how things turn out.

Student: So that's how the right idea takes on a life of its own.

Dr. Hora: Yes, that's right. The right idea takes on a life of its own and happens to be the life of God, the will of God.

Student: Well, then, the only thing that's required of us, since we can't make any decisions, is for us to pay attention.

Dr. Hora: Pay attention, listen, and respond spontaneously. You know, if you have some flowers and if you put them in this corner, they will turn this way. Do the flowers have an ego? No. They are drawn by a power that has a name: "heliotropism," which is "moving with the light." They turn toward the light. So if we seek the right responses, we have to turn toward the light. But it is not the sunlight. It is spiritual light. We are guided that way.

Now, a student asked an interesting question today. She doesn't know about it. (*Laughter*) Here is this couple, President Clinton and his beautiful, brilliant, intelligent, highly educated wife. Together they make a tremendously attractive couple. So how can it be that they have so much trouble? One trouble after another. How can good people have bad experiences, right? What do you think?

Student: Maybe it has to do with what you are saying about will, the will to do, ambition to do.

Dr. Hora: You see, it is not enough to be brilliant and beautiful and well educated and smart and a politician. It is not enough to be humanly excellent. This doesn't really count in the spiritual realm.

Human intelligence will not protect us from suffering or from troublesome experiences. Something else is more powerful, more valid, more important than all these good, admirable human qualities. What is it that is superior to all these qualities?

Student: Spiritual blessedness. Immortal mind. The Universe of Mind. The Divine Mind has a better solution than anything in the human experience, and to be able to be governed by the Divine Mind, which is supreme wisdom and love (Love-Intelligence)...that is helpful. So the trouble with the Clintons is that they are not students of Metapsychiatry. (*Laughter*)

Student: If they were, he wouldn't be President. (*Laughter*)

Student: Dr. Hora, we see the Clintons having the problems they are having. You look at President Reagan. He had a lot of forces coming after him. Somebody even shot at him, but he had the reputation of being the Teflon man. Everything rolled off of him. What is the difference in qualities?

Dr. Hora: He is not smart enough to be his own worst enemy. (*Laughter*)

Student: He was sleeping a lot.

Dr. Hora: Well, it's OK. If you are asleep, you don't hurt yourself (*laughing*).

Student: In what way are the Clintons their own worst enemy?

Dr. Hora: Because they are smart and beautiful and clever.

Student: They think they can do it.

Student: These forces are debilitating.

Dr. Hora: These qualities are human qualities. God doesn't recognize them.

Student: Neither does He recognize stupidity or ugliness. You don't have to be smart and intelligent and well educated to not be blessed.

Dr. Hora: Yes, right. Surely, surely. Only spiritual qualities count. They are the only real aspects of the enlightened life.

Student: The example that you gave earlier, where Jesus was close to the Crucifixion and he listened and he heard the answer that he had to go through with this horrendous ordeal…that's a difficult choice. How could he…I mean, in our lives we balk at smaller choices, but what does it take to follow that word and not go the other way?

Dr. Hora: In his experience, it was the Crucifixion, but many people go through horrendous experiences, and they have no remedy and they can't escape it. People are operated on, tortured, imprisoned, and murdered in Bosnia and Germany. All kinds of things. And every one of these experiences is an individual response to some situation. So we get into horrendous troubles, because we don't know what the right response is…right?

Student: So in the process that we spoke about earlier—listen, hear and respond—we wouldn't get into trouble? Is that what you mean?

Dr. Hora: Right. The Bible presents the Crucifixion as a problem that Jesus had to accept passively, in obedience to this monumental kind of request or demand. But thank God, they don't have too many crosses nowadays. There are many painful experiences that people go through, not because God wants them to but because they don't know how not to. You see, God is not a sadistic authority of some kind who enjoys watching people suffer and squirm. God is not a person. God is a cosmic reality, an intelligence. And if we have learned enough about the true nature of God, we can live in harmony with the will of God. The will of God is not like a human will. It's a condition of the universe, and when we are in harmony with the condition of the universe, we are spared suffering.

Student: Is that what you mean by "mercy" when you use that term?

Dr. Hora: Mercy, yes. Mercy is a quality of the spiritual universe. You keep asking me again and again about mercy. It is an experience of the good of God when we are released from our sense of guilt, our sense of evil, and we think we've been healed or forgiven or something like that. But let's remember that even though the Bible speaks of God as the Father, a person, and all these anthropomorphic concepts of God, God is not a person. It is hard to conceive of God in any other way, but it is possible to conceive of God as the quality of Reality. It is not a humanlike, big person or something. It is the nature of cosmic Reality, and it is vitally important to have at least an approximation of the valid view of God. If our view of God is not valid, then everything is futile, and in all our studies when we are talking about contemplation and meditation and reading and thinking of God and prayer, we are trying to find a way of bringing our awareness in line with what really is, and that's the work. When we say that prayer is the contemplation of the Truth of Being, how do you do that? Yes, it is an agonizing effort, but we can gradually, through sincere interest, approximate the truth of what God is, what man is, and what the universe is, and these three aspects of our studies have to come into line. You know, the astrologists say that this planet and that being converge at certain times. They are aligned somehow. Maybe they have something there. Our understanding of God has to reach a point that is approximately correct in any situation, and that's when we can observe mercy. When we are released from our problems, it seems like we are forgiven our sins. But God doesn't have to forgive anybody anything, because God is infinite Love-Intelligence. We have to come closer in our awareness to what God and Divine Reality are. So we have all kinds of sayings, like, for instance: "In the realm of Love-Intelligence, there is neither self nor other." Now, what makes this so important?

Student: I guess there would be no interaction. There would only be Omniaction.

Dr. Hora: Exactly. We are eliminating a very frequent problem in our thinking. The dualistic view of life is eliminated when this quotation is sincerely considered—and it is a Zen quote, by the way. The Zen master says, "In the realm of the real, there is neither self nor other. There is only that which really is." Isn't that interesting? Once you have understood that and seen the validity of this quotation, you have transcended the universal human problem of dualistic thinking. If you have transcended dualistic thinking, you have realized the nondual view of Reality, and that has brought you closer to God. God is not a psychologist. Did you know that? Psychology is evidently dualistic. It speaks of relationships of one person to another person. It's dualistic thinking. There are no relationships. And yet it seems that there are, and most people believe in them. If you watch those talk shows, there are many, many women, usually more women than men, and they always talk about meaningful relationships. They are looking for happiness in marriage and in meaningful relationships.

Student: Relationships are nothing but meaningful in psychiatric terms. These problems are fraught with meanings. It struck me as funny.

Dr. Hora: Well, that means that you have a good husband who washes the dishes for you, or something like that (*laughing*).

Student: You said that when God and man and the universe all come into alignment...I can understand that God is cosmic consciousness. I can understand that man is an individual aspect of that. What's the meaning of the symbolism of the universe coming into alignment?

Dr. Hora: The universe is a phrase pointing towards the totality of what really is. Almost everybody accepts the fact that the universe was created by God.

Student: When the universe recognizes its creator, and we as individual aspects of that recognize it with all in alignment, that's the perfect answer.

Dr. Hora: The word "universe." What does that mean? "The oneness of everything." See?

Student: I see. So an individual consciousness could recognize the oneness of everything, recognize its own aspect, and recognize the Divine creation. Then things are aligned for that one individual consciousness. And that one individual consciousness then realizes peace.

Dr. Hora: And everything good...and healings can occur because problems are not legitimate in the Reality of all things. In the universe there can be no discord, disharmony, suffering, sickness. No evil can exist in the universe. Everything has to be absolutely perfect.

Student: Then the two great commandments, "Thou shalt love the Lord thy God with all thy heart, and with all thy soul, and with all thy mind" and "Thou shalt love thy neighbor as thyself " (Matthew 22:37): Is that expressing the same idea of coming into alignment? Is loving our neighbor as our self, could that be a symbolism of the universe?

Dr. Hora: No. It is just the word connoting the right understanding of what really is. When you love your neighbor as yourself, it means that you know that your neighbor is the same as you. "To love" in a Biblical sense means "to know." In a human sense, you don't know anything, right? So you know your neighbor as you know yourself.

Student: And you know both if you follow the First Commandment, and you know that you are all part of that Divine consciousness.

Dr. Hora: You are dead already. It's good, and in our prayers, meditations, and contemplations of the truth of being, all these Biblical statements and Zen statements, and Buddhism and Taoism, they all come together. And the aim of all these studies and knowledge is to gradually conceive of Reality as nondual. The more clearly we can understand the nondual nature of Reality, the closer we are to enlightenment and to the resolution of all our conflicts and problems. "In thy presence is fulness of joy; at thy right hand there are pleasures for evermore" (Psalms 16:11). "For with thee is the light of understanding: in thy light shall we see light"[2] There are many references to this desirable thing where everything turns into one, and then comes one quote that says, "From the beginning, nothing is." He throws a monkey wrench into all these esoteric studies.

Student: What seems to be disheartening, though, is that these recognitions that I experience seem, for want of a better term, very fleeting, and it is discouraging, and I am in a constant state of insecurity as a result of that.

Dr. Hora: Yes, yes. That's true.

Student: What is that phenomenon?

Dr. Hora: As Jesus put it, the problem is judging by appearances. This oneness of the universe and all creation, it doesn't look like it is that way. (*Laughter*) It is a fantasy to judge by the way it looks, and it looks like a mess, right? (*Laughter*)

---

[2] "For with thee is the fountain of life: in thy light shall we see light" (Psalms 36:9).

Student: It's interesting. There are some humans who are trying to mess it up, and there are some humans trying to straighten it out. (*Laughter*) The ultimate dualism.

Dr. Hora: Well, we don't have to straighten out the universe. Only our consciousness and our vision have to be straight. So we are not required to fix anything. God doesn't say that. You just study to behold Reality in *your* consciousness. When your consciousness is approximating seeing the way things really are, immeasurable good can happen from it. Whatever seems to be disturbing will get straightened out, by itself. We don't have to do it. God doesn't require from us enormous effort, just sincere interest in beholding His creation, the way He created the universe and us. We are required day and night to contemplate the nature of Divine Reality and the Truth of Being—our being. Nobody else's, because if we know the truth of our being, we know the whole universe, because everyone is created by God, and that is what is required of us. No heroic efforts are required, just sincere interest. Do you remember the First Principle? Very few people remember the First Principle. (*Laughter*)

Student: I would like to ask a question, but I am not sure that I can formulate it to make sense. It seems to me that I can understand what you have been talking about today in terms of words that I know. If I would think that God is perfect, I am thinking of the words "God" and "perfect" in the context of what I have been taught in using certain vocabulary. And then if you talk about "man is an aspect of that consciousness," it is still in a particular context of words, and I would like to understand how it still seems that it is human-bound and that it isn't really what God is thinking. It's what *I* think that would be, and I don't know what God is thinking and I don't know how to…when you say we can approximate this understanding, how do you really get close to it, and how would you even know? I mean, we aren't God. So am I asking a sensible question, or…

Dr. Hora: Suppose you are thinking that 2 + 2 is 4? Who is thinking that? Are you producing these thoughts?

Student: Well, if that's a truth, then it is true, so God would be thinking that.

Dr. Hora: The truth is producing its own thought. So there is valid thinking and invalid thinking. If our thoughts acknowledge the truth of what really is, it is God in us who is thinking. If our thoughts are not valid, erroneous, false, who is thinking those thoughts? Nobody. How can nothingness think anything? Invalid thoughts are experienced as very troublesome, and yet they don't exist. Only God is the source of real thoughts. Unreal thoughts are the source of unreality. So it is nothing.

Student: But the appearance is so extraordinary as to seem otherwise.

Dr. Hora: Well, that requires us to be studying and to be able to be aware of what is and what ain't. "Is you is or is you ain't?" (*Laughing*)

Student: But you always say only God's thoughts constitute our being.

Dr. Hora: Right.

Student: But in contemplating that, it is extremely difficult to see that—God's thoughts exclusively, that's all, there is nothing else.

Dr. Hora: That's not our being. This is nothing. It's an illusion. Invalid thoughts are illusions.

Student: That also gives the appearance of duality as well, because what we are struggling with is an appearance of Divine Reality. This nothingness that seems to be something also is not supposed to be. But there seems to be this duality.

Dr. Hora: There is not really duality, because an illusion doesn't count for something.

Student: So just as we might see a mirage in the desert and recognize it as such and say, "Well that is just an illusion; there is no need for me to attempt to walk 300 miles to find water."

Dr. Hora: Right. There is no duality. Either there is water or there ain't no water. (*Laughter*)

Student: Is it that invalid thoughts can be replaced and actually displaced? Is that the point of its not being real?

Dr. Hora: Invalid thoughts cannot be replaced. Invalid thoughts disappear the moment our interest in the real thoughts takes over. Sometimes people decide they are not going to think of pink elephants, because they are invalid—nobody has ever seen pink elephants. So then you can exert a lot of energy trying not to think of pink elephants, yes? But if you said, "I am more interested in gray elephants," these pink elephants would disappear from your consciousness, from your thoughts.

Student: And by so doing, our lives are enhanced.

Dr. Hora: Yes, of course. Gray elephants are more real than pink elephants (*laughing*). It all seems very complicated, doesn't it? And yet it isn't. It's nothing. The whole thing boils down to one thing: interest. What are we really interested in? The First Principle tells you the whole of Metapsychiatry: "Thou shalt have no other interests before the good of God, which is spiritual blessedness."

The question can be asked, "How can certain thoughts be so helpful and other thoughts troublesome?" It is worth considering. What is the magic of some kinds of thoughts and the curse of other kinds of thoughts? You sit alone in a room and you think of certain thoughts, and you get very unhappy and develop all kinds of fears and pains, and if you think some other thoughts, they may heal you and set you free. It is a common experience. Anybody can say that he can understand that this happens.

There was a great concert two weeks ago in Greece, a big orchestra, and the composer stopped the music in the middle of the
concert and said, "I would like every one of you to realize one
thing: that before anything is discovered, there has to be a thought."
And then he resumed the concert and left this hanging, this
thought in people's minds. There was a profound truth in it. This
man is a philosopher. You know, the Gospel of St. John starts like
this: "In the beginning was the thought, and the thought was with
God, and the thought was God and the same thing was with God."[3]
So this idea of one thought, the power of one thought...he got this,
of course, from the Bible. But there was something very excep-
tional and beautiful when he could stop the whole big orchestra
and there was dead silence, and he came out with just this one
thing and asked people to contemplate it: Before anything can be,
there must be a thought.

---

[3] "In the beginning was the Word, and the Word was with God, and the Word was
God" (John 1:1).

2

Responding to Symptoms
of a Loved One

———   ———

Student: If we see a loved one not feeling well or complaining about a symptom, I can say that he or she is OK and is a child of God. I can think all that, but the tendency is to want to help or do something, and that is not really helpful for the individual, and I can see that. So what is required? I mean, the words are OK, but they are not real, because the temptation is there. So, what will make the difference?

Dr. Hora: It is an interesting problem. It's a paradoxical situation. When a loved one or someone you know or care for complains of symptoms, it sounds alarming. Then, according to folk wisdom, the loving thing to do is to be concerned and apply all kinds of remedies and worry and busy yourself trying to be helpful; yet the more concern you show, the more this would-be patient becomes scared and panicky and becomes convinced that his sickness is real, right? So "the good that I would I do not: but the evil which I would not, that I do" (Romans 7:19).

That is a terrible dilemma. You are a loving, beneficial presence, and there is an expectancy of becoming a beneficent person and helping people who seem to be suffering and frightened, and the more you help, the worse they get, right?

Student: I made the grave error this morning of saying, "Well, it's only a thought." He said to me, "How is that going to help me?" I said, "I'd better shut up." No matter what I said, if it wasn't filled with concern, it wasn't going to be helpful. (*Laughter*)

Dr. Hora: Yes. If you are filled with concern, it gets worse. It gets much worse. Isn't that crazy?

Student: And compounding the problem is the fact that when those close to us are ill, very often it's based on interaction thoughts with *us*. (*Laughter*)

Dr. Hora: That's right. The helpee hates the helper, and the harder the helper tries to help, the worse everything goes.

I once saw an old French comedy film. A man started to have a little cough, and the people around him became very lovingly helpful to him, and he started vomiting. Then they took his temperature, and it shot up high. They brought towels to put over his head, and pretty soon he had pneumonia, and the doctors came, and he got worse, and they called the ambulance, and they took him to the hospital, and there were more helpful people around, and at one point this guy said, "What the hell are you doing?" He got fed up with all of this help, got out of his bed, put on his clothes, and left and ran away from this culture of concerned, beneficent persons. Now, if there is some unfriendly consciousness in this room, it will ask, "What are you saying, Dr. Hora? Do you want us to be callous and uncaring and cruel, and not give a damn about people suffering?"

So, what is a Good Samaritan to do? In the Bible (Luke 10:29-37) there was a good Samaritan who passed by a man who had been mugged, and he really helped him and bound up his wounds and took this guy to a hotel. He paid for his room and said to the hotel keeper, "You take care of him. I have to go away, but I will pay you in advance for whatever care you are going to provide him," and he left. What do you think of that? He was helpful, but he wasn't making a fuss over him, and he wasn't taking credit for helping. He was just naturally doing what makes sense to do, and he had enough money to pay for his care. He left, and the victim never knew who it was. In other words his assistance was nonpersonal—not emotional, not hysterical. He was just a beneficial presence without any interpersonal relationship developing between the helper and the helpee. He wasn't hysterical over the situation; neither was he callous. He was loving, but he was loving the right way. What is the right love, the perfect love? When you go home tonight, do you know how to love perfectly?

Student: It all depends on how much complaining there is. (*Laughter*)

Dr. Hora: Nonpersonal, nonconditional benevolence. That is the right kind of helpfulness: nonpersonal, nonconditional benevolence. Now, what's wrong with telling a loved one who is not a student of Metapsychiatry, "Ah it's just a thought"? (*Laughter*) He will pick up the book *Beyond the Dream* and throw it at you. (*Laughter*) You see how hard it is to be a beneficial presence? But if they happen to be students of Metapsychiatry, you can tell them, "Look here, Hora says it's only a thought." (*Laughter*)

OK, so much for being helpful. It's not easy to be helpful the right way. One has to really understand perfect love. "Perfect love casteth out fear" (1 John 4:18). Human concern and helpfulness increase fear. The moment you start fussing over somebody, the fear increases. But if you understand perfect love, there is no fear, so the suffering individual has a chance to see the situation in the right light and can recover quickly. I hope you all can see the difference.

Student: Well the *concerned* individual is fearful.

Dr. Hora: Of course he is fearful. Sure.

Student: So if the concerned individual sees that it's only a thought and keeps his or her mouth shut (*laughter*)—I guess I don't understand what it means to comfort someone in that way, because to them, the symptom is real.

Dr. Hora: Comfort is very frightening.

Student: Because comforting is concern.

Dr. Hora: Yes. It's confirmation that the picture is real and that it has the potential of getting worse.

Student: So if we are clear in consciousness that it's only a thought and there is no fear at all, then somehow that message is conveyed.

Dr. Hora: Perfect love will heal the situation—nonpersonal, nonconditional benevolence.

Student: When you are close to a person, it would be hard to have perfect love, because basically you are afraid that maybe they are going to die. You have an attachment and feel very frightened, and then there is panic. So what do you do?

Dr. Hora: If the helper is panicky, imagine how frightening it must be for the helpee. It's terrible. You can't afford to be frightened. The fear must be cast out of the helper, which occurs if you know that everything and everyone is perfect in the sight of God under all circumstances and you understand the perfect love, which casts out fear.

Student: Short of understanding perfect love, might it also be helpful to understand the concept of compassion?

Dr. Hora: Oh, it couldn't hurt. (*Laughter*) Yes, but not to be confused with sympathy, empathy, antipathy, and pity. No pity. We are pitiless.

Student: That seems very difficult, because if someone we know has died, let's say a tragic death, which seems to happen frequently—to that individual, it's a great loss. Because they are not enlightened in any way, they suffer greatly by this loss even though we know that that's really not necessary. But then it seems like it's difficult to understand an appropriate response. I mean you can't ignore the fact that they had this loss. You have to say something to them.

Dr. Hora: You are not talking about the one who died.

Student: No, I am talking about the one who suffered the loss.

Dr. Hora: You are speaking of someone who is afflicted by grief.

Student: Yes.

Dr. Hora: Is that it?

Student: Yes...so would compassion be the only appropriate response?

Dr. Hora: Well, compassion, of course, is a wonderful, healing quality of someone who is loving and truly helpful. But then you are saying there is a condition, the human experience of grief, that is like a disease—a very strong, powerful, very painful disease—a painful experience. Would you like to ask us now what the helpful attitude is toward someone who is suffering from grief?

Student: Yes, that is exactly what I need.

Dr. Hora: Who can help us with that problem? Grief is a very serious experience, and psychoanalysis has complex explanations about the process of grief, and it recommends that it must be allowed to work itself out in an individual, and it takes time. This is called "the work of mourning." You have to give an individual a chance to mourn, and sometimes this mourning process is protracted and takes a long time. Now the question is—that's the psychoanalytic view. Isn't there a better way to benefit someone in the condition of grief? Good grief! How can anybody say that about grief, that it's "good grief"?

Do you know what Jesus said about grief? He said, "Blessed are they that mourn: for they shall be comforted" (Matthew 5:4). What could he have meant? Was he a psychoanalyst recommending that people mourn?

Student: It probably requires us to refocus our attention. In times of mourning, just like with any other problem, we have the tendency to turn toward God. If we are in the process of mourning, we have great pain, so it is an opportunity to learn something.

Dr. Hora: That's interesting. Could you somehow clarify what you mean by "turn to God"?

Student: Like myself. Whenever I have a difficult problem, those are the times when I am more apt to read *Beyond the Dream* than when times are OK.

Dr. Hora: You are an unusual fellow. Most people aggravate their experience of pain through thinking, *I am justified in feeling sorry for myself, because I suffered this great loss.* This is normal reasoning. If you reason this way, you can make a federal case out of your grief, and after a while you can learn to like it, too. Then you develop a facial attitude that tells the world, "You have to be nice to me. You have to be sympathetic to me. You have to give me what I want, because I am grieving, and there is nothing anyone can say." Therefore, people say, "We feel sorry for you, we feel with you, we express our condolences for you, and we understand that this is very painful to you." We treat the grieving individual with kid gloves. Now, what happens when we do that?

Student: It probably becomes self-confirmatory for them, and then they enjoy it.

Dr. Hora: Exactly.

Student: It would also prevent any opportunity for them to see anything at all that might be helpful.

Dr. Hora: Except themselves. Right. OK. So, we here are not interested in being psychoanalytically sophisticated people. We are seeking, looking to Jesus Christ to show us a better way. When Jesus resurrected Lazarus from the grave, the family was in mourning, greatly grieved. What did he say? He said, "Loose him, and let him go" (John 11:44). What a strange thing to say. And when the philosopher Heidegger was asked about mourning, he gave a definition. He said, "Mourning is remaining with the dead." What does that mean?

Student: You are too attached to the person.

Dr. Hora: Right. You cling, and you remain mentally preoccupied with the fact that you have lost somebody. You have lost somebody, and you feel sorry for yourself. You ruminate over it: *How could it have happened to me, this tragedy?* Jesus said, "Loose him, and let him go." Don't be stuck in the grave with the dead one or whatever else. You have to loose him and let him go. What's that?

Student: Lazarus's family was very attached to him.

Dr. Hora: Exactly. The more possessive we are, the more painful the grief experience is, because the greater the sense of loss. Have you ever lost a cat or a dog that you got attached to? Loose him and let him go. We have to stop thinking about the individual or object or whatever we have lost. How is it possible to do that?

Student: Something that seems to be helpful is that instead of focusing on the person as a possession of material substance, to focus on him or her as an individual spiritual being, never beginning, never ending.

Dr. Hora: You cannot lose such an individual Divine consciousness. That is what is meant by "turning to God." What happens when we turn to God in an understanding way?

Student: We are healed.

Dr. Hora: Yes, but how could we explain that?

Student: You turn away from the transitory aspects of the individual — the body, the appearance — to the enduring aspects, the eternal aspects and spiritual qualities.

Dr. Hora: In addition to that, we abandon the error of interaction thinking. There is neither self nor other; there is just the infinite presence of Divine Love-Intelligence. The more we understand this, the shorter the period of mourning, because we allow the light of Divine Reality to enter into the tomb. As Jesus entered into the tomb where Lazarus had been lying dead for four days, he brought with him the light of life, and he said, "Lazarus, come out. Get up and come out of here"—and he came out. He was bound with swaddling cloth. He was bound up; he couldn't move. I don't know how he came out of it (*laughter*), but it has symbolic meaning. The possessive family tied him up so much that he couldn't live anymore. They were so clutching at him and loving him so possessively, he had to die. Jesus knew that, so he awakened Lazarus and told his family to loose him and let him go. Then he could live.

Student: I don't understand "Blessed are they that mourn: for they shall be comforted" when considering the other definition of mourning as "remaining with the dead."

Dr. Hora: If you mourn the right way, this is a very enlightening experience, because it highlights Divine Reality as never born and never dying, hid with Christ in God. You begin to see there is more to life than the body. It helps people to open up to Divine consciousness, and it's a great comfort.

Student: Isn't there something in the Bible that says there is a specific period to mourn, and after that the mourning shall cease?

Dr. Hora: Various religions have certain rituals of mourning. I think the Irish mourn by partying. It is called an Irish wake.

Student: In the Jewish religion, there are seven days of mourning, and they have company and food. When my father passed away, I asked my mother, "Why are they celebrating?" She said, "You are not supposed to be sad when someone passes away, or they will never rest."

Dr. Hora: There are traditions and ways of trying to comfort people who are in this painful experience. There is nothing wrong with it.

Student: Basically, mourning seems selfish. I really suffered a loss. I had a dog. Was I mourning the loss of the dog, or was I mourning the loss of what the dog meant to me when I would come home every night? What the dog meant to me is what I miss, what I mourn.

Dr. Hora: Yes.

Student: So is the grieving individual ruminating over the tragic death that the close one suffered or actually ruminating over how he or she feels?

Dr. Hora: It's inevitable, because we interpret our experiences in personal terms. I have heard people express a lot of hostility toward the one that died. "How could he do this to me?" You may have heard this.

Let us talk about something good. (*Laughter*)

Student: I'd like to ask a question about the original question. You said perfect love is the answer to the question asked at the beginning. How does that translate into action? I understand all the things that would *not* be helpful, but I don't understand as clearly what *is* helpful. It seems correct that it would be perfect love, but I don't know how to translate it into action.

Dr. Hora: What makes you think action is necessary?

Student: I don't know.

Dr. Hora: It's a perfectly human kind of assumption that only action and activity is real. If you don't do anything, then you don't do anything, and nothing can happen. The idea is, if you don't do something, who will do it?

Student: There is a social expectation that you are expected to do certain things or act a certain way when somebody says that he or she is sick.

Dr. Hora: Sure, and the more you do it, the worse it will get.

Student: Is it possible to just see what's needed?

Dr. Hora: What's needed? The Chinese sage says that there is such a thing as action that is nonaction. What did he mean? Certainly perfect love doesn't do anything. The beneficent person is a normal human being who is convinced that to express love you have to do something or heal somebody or perform certain rituals. But perfect love doesn't have to do anything, because it *is*; it is that which already is. Interestingly enough, the doer doesn't accomplish much, but the nondoer, whose consciousness is filled with perfect love, doesn't have to do anything, because this perfect love is present, is omnipotent. It is real. Reality doesn't need to do anything. Reality already is, and God saw everything He had made and behold, it was very good. If there is perfect love in a situation, nothing has to be done. This love accomplishes whatever is needed: the healing, the elevation of the consciousness, the relief from whatever is burdensome. It is a spiritual force that harmonizes all situations and heals all problems without moving a finger.

Now consider the Buddha statue in the office. You have all seen this. He sits cross-legged. Why is he sitting cross-legged? He is saving the world. He is a beneficial presence in the world, and he is not doing anything. He just sits there. He doesn't even talk. He doesn't move. How can he do nothing? Doesn't he have to do something? No. He *is*, and those who understand his message are healed or liberated from all discordant experiences in their lives, because it's the power of God that is emanating from that consciousness. That's what the world needs.

Student: When a loved one says he or she is sick, are you talking about us or are you talking about them? Are we always working on ourselves? What are you talking about when you say this? Are we praying about ourselves when we are presented with this?

Dr. Hora: Yes. We are praying to become fully conscious of perfect love. Perfect love is the power of God present in us and around us. Anyone who is able to understand and be conscious of perfect love, by his sheer presence, will see good things happen. It's hard to understand. How is anything going to happen if you are not doing anything, right?

Student: Is there some sort of realization by the person that was healed, on his or her part?

Dr. Hora: Not necessarily. They just find they are suddenly well.

Student: The sickness is a manifestation of a problem that they have.

Dr. Hora: Yes. It's usually lack of love. It is an interesting thing for all of you to consider. In our culture and everywhere in the world, there is an idea that we have to love one another. Even Jesus said, "Love one another; as I have loved you" (John 13:34). When we try to love one another, what do we do? We start working on our relationships. We try to improve our relationships with people to such an extent that it feels like we are all loving. We hug and we kiss and we pet and we give gifts and we do everything we know how to improve our relationship with someone in an effort to be loving. Some people do this all their lives and work hard at it, especially if they are psychologically indoctrinated—the wife, and husband, the family member who is sophisticated in psychological thinking, will work assiduously to produce a good relationship. It's very normal, natural. Everybody does it. Now, what happens when we work hard to achieve a good relationship in order that we can *feel* that we are loving? What happens? There is no love there. We may come to the realization that we have deceived ourselves into believing that this way we can have a loving relationship. How long does this loving relationship last? Not very long. Pretty soon it turns sour.

I like to compare this to people who are trying to become wealthy, so what they do is collect nine-dollar bills—lots of nine-dollar bills. They think that if they have enough nine-dollar bills, they will be wealthy. So they do this. They collect these nine-dollar bills believing that they will feel rich, and then they discover that this is not real currency. It was a mistake. Similarly, working on a relationship in order to become loving is also a mistake. You don't get rich with nine-dollar bills, and you don't become a loving individual by working on your relationships. Isn't that interesting? You can't become a loving individual by working hard on improving your relationships. Similarly, you cannot become rich by collecting nine-dollar bills, but the Bible recommends that we must become loving. "God is love, and he that dwelleth in love dwelleth in God, and God in him" (1 John 4:16). You can't produce God by relationships. The Bible doesn't recommend that you work on your relationships and then you will become loving. It won't work. Are you surprised? So, how do we become loving?

Student: I notice that whether someone is sick or we're working on a relationship, it's our tendency to want to do something.

Dr. Hora: It's the human condition. When we consider the statue of the Buddha, we see that it is really manifesting perfect love. So, how do we become loving if we cannot do it? "There is no fear in love; but perfect love casteth out fear.... He that feareth is not made perfect in love" (1 John 4:18), but "God is love; and he that dwelleth in love dwelleth in God and God in him (1 John 4:16)," It doesn't say interpersonal relationships make love. Nine-dollar bills will not make a fortune. In order to become loving, we have to dwell in God. How do we dwell in God?

Student: By manifesting the qualities of God.

Dr. Hora: How do you do that? Can you do this?

Student: No, but you can understand it. You can realize it.

Dr. Hora: What does it mean to dwell in God? To dwell in God means to be mindful of the true nature of God as love, perfect love. We have the great blessing of having been given the correct definition of perfect love. What is perfect love?

Student: Nonconditional, nonpersonal benevolence.

Dr. Hora: So we contemplate and appreciate perfect love by knowing the difference between perfect love and personal relationships. We cannot manipulate our interpersonal relationships into a loving state—this is just phony baloney. It will not work. It's counterfeit. Interpersonal "love" is as counterfeit as a nine-dollar bill. So we have to learn what love really is and how it can be realized. We need to learn to dwell in God, that God dwells in us, and that God is love. We make this an object of our meditations, contemplations, and desire. We have this desire to realize perfect love. And it happens. When consciousness is imbued with this Reality, this truth, wonderful things can happen— instant healings.

There is a saying in folklore, "Don't take any wooden nickels." Remember that? We say, "Don't take any nine-dollar bills. It won't get you rich."

Student: There was a situation today. We went on a class trip, and I noticed a father had come along with us, and a young woman who had been a student teacher also came along. I noticed at one point that there was one girl who clung physically, whenever she could, to the student teacher. There was another girl who clung physically to the father (who wasn't her father) whenever she could. I watched them and observed this. What is the meaning of these children literally physically clinging to these individuals?

Dr. Hora: Some people like to cling. They are called the Klingons. (*Laughter*)

Student: The adults seemed to like it also. They liked being clung on to.

Student: Is that their idea of love?

Dr. Hora: Possessive love. There is such a thing as possessive love, which is not really love. It's just a stranglehold. What is a "solitary man"? Can you think of a model of a solitary man?

Student: Daniel.

Dr. Hora: Daniel—and Jesus also. But Jesus didn't claim to be a man, but the Son of God; however, Daniel was free to move about, and he was always with God. A solitary man doesn't cling to his fellow man. He is always with God, and that gives him the greatest possible freedom to live his life the best possible way. There are loners who are afraid of people, there are lonely people who long for companionship, and then there are gregarious people who always want to socialize. But real freedom can be had only if one is a solitary man.

3

Awareness vs. Thinking;
Love and Reverence; Sincerity

Student: Dr. Hora, I know we say emotions are thoughts. So are emotions in Metapsychiatry treated as symptoms where we would ask the meaning? Like, say, if we feel bad, is it the same as symptoms?

Dr. Hora: Yes. Symptoms are also thoughts. So thoughts can appear in the form of feelings, emotions, dreams, or physical symptoms. Everything begins with a thought. "In the beginning was the thought, and the thought was with God...and the thought was God," and that's all that was in the beginning. "...[T]he light shineth in darkness and darkness comprehended it not."[4] And that is where we are.

Student: It is good to know that it is thought; otherwise, it is possible to get very involved with an emotion.

Dr. Hora: Sure. Occasionally people ask a student of Metapsychiatry, "Are you still going to see this man Hora, and why are you going to see him?" And the answer is that Metapsychiatry is too simple to comprehend. (*Laughter*) The complex things, people pick up quickly. You pick up this complicated process called computer

---

[4] "In the beginning was the Word, and the Word was with God, and the Word was God...And the light shineth in darkness; and the darkness comprehended it not." (John 1:1-5)

science. I am amazed how many people can learn it, very well, quickly. But Metapsychiatry is too simple. We are not prepared to understand what is simple. It is very paradoxical, of course. The simplicity of Metapsychiatry is expressed in one sentence: "All is infinite mind and its infinite manifestations, and that's all there is." Everything else is complicated, so people are going for it. People are studying *A Course in Miracles.* Two big volumes, and they are studying and studying and studying. It is very complicated, and the more you study, the more you don't know. The miracles are not happening, but the miracle is that you keep studying it. It is the simplicity of the Truth that is difficult.

Student: Is it that there is a greater interest in intellectual pursuits?

Dr. Hora: Absolutely. You want to figure it out. You want to feel that you are smart.

Student: We're not? (*Laughter*)

Dr. Hora: You do not have to be smart to become enlightened. You just have to be sincere, and that is difficult. To most people, it is very difficult to be sincere.

Student: In regard to the question about emotion: In one of your first books, you had emotionalism as one of the "five gates of hell." Being that it is so prevalent in human consciousness to be emotional—

Dr. Hora: You are asking why there is emotionalism?

Student: No, I am asking how you get beyond it. Because it seems so prevalent, and to actually live without emotions, beyond emotionalism, seems a pretty big step to take in this lifetime, because so much is based on "what I felt"—*I felt this, I felt that.*

Dr. Hora: Emotionalism and feelings are no problem at all once you have the courage to admit that you are dealing with thoughts. Then there is no problem. It is very simple. Again, who will accept a simple answer? Ask a psychologist about emotions. Boy, libraries are filled with explanations of what emotions are—and feelings— oh, oh, oh, feelings. (*Laughter*) The luckiest people are the people who like people. (*Laughter*) You see what happens to people that complicate life by not understanding? Nobody asks, "What *are* emotions? What *are* feelings?" No, it is assumed that this *is* and that you have to learn to handle it. Psychology teaches you how to handle your emotions and your feelings and your relationships, and you are messing around in nothingness—absolute nothingness. So how do you *feel* about this, and how do you *feel* about that? How do you *feel* about the Bosnians and about the Palestinians, and how do you *feel* about the Clinton policy? All kinds of questions that just complicate life and don't face up to it—feelings are just simply thoughts. You have to know what you are thinking, and then you can separate out the valid thoughts from the invalid thoughts, and the whole process is very simple.

Student: The mind is so perverted, because it doesn't allow us to see the simplicity. Quite often there is something I have been holding on to for years, and then you say, "No, no, no," and I say, "But, but, but…" (*Dr. Hora laughs.*) There is such a resistance to accepting it. I understand it is only thought, yet there has been an investment in it.

Dr. Hora: Right. There is a famous story about a Zen master who was planning to die because he was very old, and there was a lot of politics going on in his school about who would be the successor, and everybody was voting for the most brilliant student in that school. They were vying and competing with each other, formulating the answer to the question *What is Zen?* They wrote treatises and all kinds of poems, and everybody was very uptight about who would be the successor of the master. When it came to the point of appointing the successor, the master said, "The dishwasher in the kitchen. He is the most enlightened guy among you all." They were flabbergasted. He never even attended the lectures (*laughing*)! But he certainly was more enlightened than anybody else, because he had a simple, forthright, sincere understanding of the Truth. And that is what is needed.

Student: So how do we develop an appreciation for the simplicity of it? Because there is this tendency to look for complexity.

Dr. Hora: That is why they invented the bamboo pole. (*Laughter*)

Student: It seems like there are two things going on at the same time. When you talk about the simplicity, I understand what you are saying, and I can appreciate that. Then when problems are discussed here and meanings are clarified, it seems to me there is so much to know, it would take several lifetimes. There is always something either in the group or in private session that comes up that seems—first you recognize how important the clarification of the issue is. It all seems very complicated. It isn't—it is very simple—but there are these two things going on. I can't seem to get it clear, whether it's simple or complicated. (*Laughter*) I told Dr. Hora today about an experience I had, and it was very simple, and he clarified it. But it seems like there are so many things that you have to understand in order to be here for God.

Dr. Hora: Why "so many things"?

Student: I don't know. It seems difficult.

Student: On the natural level with learning, it appears the one who really knows and understands can very simply teach or allow for the learning. It's the one who really knows it, and knows all the parameters, who then can present it very simply. Enough said.

Dr. Hora: What is there to know?

Student: I guess with a math problem, a person who really understands that area of math, fractions or whatever it may be, and really has the wholeness of the concept, can present it simply. Whereas people who know parts and pieces of it will give a more fractured kind of presentation. Sometimes the whole idea will eventually be expressed, but it is the one who has the insight in the first place who presents it best.

Dr. Hora: She will be the successor of the Zen master. (*Laughter*) I guess that is how they were speculating when it came to choosing a successor.

Student: It has also been said about the Truth that it is like a pearl necklace. If you understand one idea perfectly, like picking up only one pearl in the strand, you can grasp the entire necklace—

Dr. Hora: When you pull it out from the toilet (*laughing*).

Student: At one place I had a teacher whom students really wanted as a teacher because they felt they really learned a lot. In talking with him about this, he said that what he did was concentrate on one piece of literature and really know it from all perspectives. He taught it many times, but by knowing this well, everything else fit in.

Dr. Hora (*to another student*)*:* Why are you laughing?

Student: Well, as an example, today Dr. Hora helped me see that the meaning of a bad experience I had was that I had been thinking that I know and that somebody else doesn't. He told me that what is needed is reverence for life. I was just walking to the car and putting money in the meter, and I was thinking, *If you could live that way, that statement is the answer to everything. If you have reverence for life, there are no problems with anything.* It covers every problem that was ever brought up here, right? So that is very simple. Last week, the last thing you said to me was that if I didn't learn perfect love, then all the years that I have spent here will be wasted. Now, that statement…when I left here, I thought, *There is only one statement, and that covers everything. That's it. There is nothing that doesn't fall right in there.* So I remember those two. Probably the week before there was another thing. So the last thing you said to me seems to cover everything. But I don't know. On the one hand, it seems very simple. On the other hand, it seems like after 50 years of these kinds of statements, it seems very complicated (*laughing*).

Dr. Hora: She is trying to explain. She had a problem with an oil delivery man, the truck driver. She had just heard about reverence for life, but when the truck driver pulled up with this big oil truck, who the hell would think about reverence for life? (*Laughter*) Then the idea is, *Let's make sure that nothing gets damaged.* Right? So we don't think about reverence for life. The concept "reverence for life" is beautiful, and everybody can like it and accept it. It makes a lot of sense, but people don't apply it. It is just theory. Reverence for life has to become one aspect of our mode of being-in-the-world. Then it is always there when it is needed. It works by itself. We don't have to make it work. If when the truck arrived, she had had the thought *This truck driver is a creation of God...he has the intelligence of God...he is a transparency for God...he knows how to drive a truck...*if she would have reasoned that way, the problem would not have developed. But she was thinking about practical ways of how to prevent this stupid truck driver from damaging the parking area. Right? So, you see, it is not practical. It's not complicated. It's very simple. But who can live like that? First one has to be enlightened, and then one doesn't have to remind oneself to apply it, as a technique, to truck driving. In everything, man complicates his thought processes and his thinking, preferring to be complicated.

Student: I think you just answered my question. But I was going to ask, do we forget, or is it that we just really never understood it in the first place?

Dr. Hora: The trouble is that we think that we are thinkers.

Student: We think we understand, but we really don't understand.

Dr. Hora: We are thinking. Now, many people will say, "Well, do you recommend that we become nonthinkers, stupid and glorifying ignorance?" We are not against thinking. We are *for* awareness. Now, in what way is awareness different from thinking?

Student: When you are in a state of awareness, you are aware that everything is thought. There is invalid and valid thought. There is a heightened sense of awareness and discernment, so you can see you are awake.

Dr. Hora: That is a pretty good explanation. Is there something else you wanted to say?

Student: I was just going to say that then we can allow for God's thoughts to obtain in consciousness.

Dr. Hora: That's right. God is the only thinker. But we have to pay attention to what God is thinking. How do you do that?

Student: We have to somehow lose interest in being a thinker.

Dr. Hora: Absolutely. Is that possible? (*Laughter*) It is not possible. We cannot lose it, but we can become oriented toward awareness rather than thinking. Now, in the realm of mathematics and computer science you cannot work with awareness. You have to think.

Student: No, not completely. There are many situations in which one is puzzled with no solution, and then it comes if you are receptive.

Dr. Hora: Yes, that's right. So the human condition itself is a great distraction and confusion. How to be an enlightened human being? The answer is you have to be a dishwasher in a Zen school for a few years. (*Laughter*)

Student: How do we lose interest in being a thinker?

Dr. Hora: By shifting our interest to the good of God, which is spiritual blessedness, and one aspect of spiritual blessedness is inspired wisdom from moment to moment. We are available for the Divine Mind to speak to us and give us ideas that are needed for every moment. This is the inspired way of functioning. Then there are the calculative thinkers who have been brought up to figure everything out in their brains. Brain children.

I heard a story about a skiing accident where two skiers collided and they got hurt, and one of the skiers started yelling, "Why don't you use your left brain?" See, psychologists came to a dead end with their "brainology," so they invented that there is a left brain and there is a right brain. You have heard of that, yes? And now if things don't work out, they blame it on some people thinking with the left brain and the other people thinking with the right brain. Metapsychiatry says it's all hogwash (*laughing*). There is no such thing. Intelligence doesn't come from the brain. It is from the Divine Mind, and it is all one. If you give people such an idea that there is the left brain and the right brain, they will write very erudite treatises, lectures, and books, but nothing happens in their lives; they just struggle trying to figure things out. Some people have even developed courses about teaching the left-brain people how to use the right brain and the right-brain people how to use the left brain. This is very knowledgeable and very scientific. Have you heard this recently? Suddenly it fades away, and people don't struggle anymore. In Metapsychiatry, there is no such thing. There is only God. God is infinite intelligence and love, and when you love, you have all the wisdom of God available to you in the right moment. It is an inspired mode of being in the world. It is neither anatomical nor physiological. It is spiritual.

Student: When that big truck started to pull up, I assume on her lawn, the first thing that happens is you think invalid thoughts: *There is this dumb truck driver and this big truck, and it's ruining my lawn*—and at that moment, what a blessing if you can pray.

Dr. Hora: You have to pray even before that.

Student: Before the truck arrives. But it's so difficult, Dr. Hora, to forget everything you have ever heard, ever learned, ever understood or thought you understood.

Dr. Hora: You don't have to forget anything, because everything that you are trying to forget is nothing. What is needed is interest. Now tell me, what will happen if you interview a thousand people who are spiritually minded, and they take all kinds of courses like "A Course in Miracles" and Zen and spiritual courses, and they go to lectures—if you ask them what the difference is between wanting to get enlightened and being interested in the good of God? Isn't that a fair question? Who will get enlightened first? The one that wants very much to get enlightened or the other one, who is interested? There could be a thousand students of spiritual teachings, and how many will know the answer? You may not find many, even among students of Metapsychiatry. Who can explain it? Who can tell you why? (*Laughter*)

Student: The idea that self-confirmatory ideation is troublesome is not very widespread.

Dr. Hora: Right. Can you explain the difference between wanting to be enlightened and being interested in enlightenment?

Student: The latter, being interested in enlightenment, is really being interested in the Truth, and one transcends the self through that.

Dr. Hora: How is that?

Student: Because the issue is understanding, and there isn't any ulterior motive than to know what is real, whereas the other, the wanting, is self-glorifying to a certain extent. There is a component of self-confirmation and self-glorification. Wanting to be enlightened and to be known as being enlightened, etc.

Dr. Hora: Anybody else?

Students: Interest is love, and wanting is personal.

Dr. Hora: Interest is love, and wanting is personal, willful, and arrogant, which in itself defeats the purpose immediately. If you don't know the difference, you can never become enlightened. It's so subtle. It is so important to understand the subtlety of these two ways of looking at the situation. The more we want, the less there is the possibility to really become enlightened. You cannot want it. But if you are sincerely interested, you are loving, you are receptive—by the grace of God, it comes to you. It's like catching pigeons, right? Remember some years ago I was teaching you how to catch pigeons. Can you remember? How do we catch pigeons? You don't remember? My teaching was in vain. (*Laughter*) How do we catch pigeons?

Student: Patiently. (*Laughter*)

Dr. Hora: Something more is needed. You sit quietly with some bread or some food, and they will settle down and they will come to you. But if you are willful and *want* to catch them, you will never catch them. That is what I was teaching one of you about 15 years ago. (*Laughter*) She still doesn't know how to catch pigeons. (*Laughter*) You see, studying Metapsychiatry is very simple but very difficult at the same time.

Student: What is the definition of enlightenment?

Dr. Hora: Enlightenment is knowing God. That's all. You have to know God. You have to know what God is, who God is…how old is He, where does He live, how does He operate, when is His birthday? (*Laughing*)

Student: That's important, I guess, because most intellectuals don't ask themselves. They say, "I want enlightenment," and it sort of implies you know what you want and what it is.

Dr. Hora: You have to know what you want, and you go after it (*laughing*). So you could say enlightenment is very easy. It's like catching pigeons, right?

Student: Isn't there a wanting to catch the pigeon?

Dr. Hora: If there is a wanting, then it will never happen.

Student: You just *allow* it to happen?

Dr. Hora: Allow? How do you allow?

Student: You have the bread and allow the pigeon to come.

Dr. Hora: "Allow the pigeon to come." What do you think of that?

Student: It is arrogant to allow things to happen.

Dr. Hora: It is a very important differentiation: When you allow a pigeon to come, the pigeon says, "Go to hell. You don't love me. I am afraid of you." You never catch a pigeon by allowing it to come. Did you know that?

Student: We have a cat at work.

Dr. Hora: The cat will catch the pigeon. (*Laughter*)

Student: I would like the cat to come to me, but she doesn't. She goes to somebody else who has cats at home or—whatever the reason, she doesn't come to me. It's very interesting. Perhaps because I want her to come is one reason, one possibility.

Dr. Hora: What makes the cat or the pigeon come?

Student: Love.

Dr. Hora: Of course. Love.

Student: I love the cat.

Dr. Hora: You love pigeons? They come. You don't chase after them. You don't lay a trap. You don't ask the janitor to do it for you. So it is not a matter of allowing. Allowing is not love. It is just a clever ploy. You allow the pigeon to come—no, you have to have reverence for the life of the pigeon. You love the pigeons, and you offer them some food, and they come because you love them. Love is interest. Allowing is not love, right? Do your cats know how to catch pigeons? This is not just linguistic refinement we are talking about. We are talking about existential attunement, *at-one-ment,* with another life form. There are people who attract tigers, wild animals. They come. My housekeeper, Rita, feeds the deer. We have thousands of deer. (*Laughter*) She feeds all the wild animals in the neighborhood. They come every evening at 6:00 in the back of the house because they know that she has prepared food for them for dinner, and they clean it up. There is nothing left to clean up after them. They eat everything. There are all kinds of animals that come and eat what she prepares for them. The deer come for the apples. We have an apple orchard. She spreads these apples for them. They all come. It's like the Serengeti plain around that house now. (*Laughter*) She loves these animals, and they come to her. The secret is the love, not letting. Letting is not love. It's just "To hell with it, you can have it if you want to," or something like that. So you have to love. You are receptive. You are affirming their value when you have the right attitude, and they know it.

Student: And they know somehow that she doesn't want anything in return for the love that she is giving them.

Dr. Hora: She loves them naturally; she loves animals. When I appear at the window of our living room, they run away. (*Laughter*) She is always taking pictures of these animals. They come. They stay.

They sleep. They pose for her. She has a whole series of pictures of the deer looking into the window.

Student: What tremendous implications this all has for transcending interaction. It's interaction thinking that is the basis for all the problems. It's astounding to consider it.

Dr. Hora: Sure.

Student: If this communicates itself without any words—it just communicates itself—then it communicates itself to other people, and if somebody knows that you have reverence for life, the life they are manifesting, there would be no interaction, no invalid thoughts.

Dr. Hora: Of course. There is only omniaction. Omniaction is the presence of God manifesting itself in goodness, in healings, in harmony.

Student: And sickness would disappear.

Dr. Hora: Never, never occur.

Student: So with that in mind, with what we were talking about earlier, if we understand perfect love, then that is the ultimate understanding, and everything else follows. Reverence for life. These are just all aspects of the main thing, which is perfect love.

Dr. Hora: Yes. Sure.

Student: So, then, when we present a problem, you give us the right thoughts for that particular problem. But you've always talked a lot about the four "Ws," because that realigns us with the Truth.

Dr. Hora: I haven't talked about it recently. I have assumed that you know it. (*Laughter*) But I may be wrong.

Student: I don't think you should assume things. (*Laughter*)

Student: I guess there is an element of truth in that, too. That seems to be the ultimate truth, so that if you know the four "Ws," then you are enlightened.

Dr. Hora: Of course.

Student: So when you say love is interest, it is interest in seeing the good of God manifest? That's the interest?

Dr. Hora: Of course, and the method of making progress on this path is sincere contemplation of the good of God. Very simple, right? You don't have to read heavy books and burden your head with it. Sincere contemplation of the good of God. The other day somebody was complaining, "Dr. Hora, I have been studying Metapsychiatry for so many years, and I still don't know it." So I said, "Have you already learned how to be sincere?" Of course not. She is lying all the time and manipulating and asking leading questions. There are some people who think they are asking questions, but they are just pressuring for an answer, and they already have in their mind how it should come out. These are the people who are asking leading questions. That is also a very bad form of insincerity.

Student: So if nothing is happening in our lives, and we think we know or we see ourselves thinking, then that is an indication there is a lack of sincerity?

Dr. Hora: Very often that is a big stumbling block in studying Metapsychiatry: an inability to be really sincere. Because the questioner always has in the back of his mind that he is going to get the right answer. If only he is clever enough to ask the right way, then Hora will give the answer he wants to hear. One student kept pressuring me to tell her whether she should bring her mother from New York to California, and I refused to fall for this. Week after week, in a hundred ways, she would approach it, trying to get me to say whether she should bring her mother to California or not. The assumption was that I knew. I never told her that I knew what was good for her mother, and I kept saying, "What is good for you is to learn sincerity and not to ask leading questions." She didn't like that. That was very frustrating. Sincerity is perhaps the most difficult. Insincerity, operationalism, and interaction—these bad habits of thought become great stumbling blocks. And of course I left out self-righteousness. When they pressure you to acknowledge that they know and that they are right, these are the stumbling blocks that make the learning process very difficult.

Student: I didn't know that. What blocks sincerity? What would get in the way?

Dr. Hora: What blocks sincerity? It is a desire to influence people. *How to Win Friends and Influence People.* Do you remember this famous, successful book? It is utterly wrong. The assumption is totally wrong, and a big authority wrote this and made a million dollars and more on it. Everybody bought it, because if he tells you how to win friends and influence people, you will be successful. And he was very successful. But of course it is wrong. You can tell whether a proposition is valid or not by the number of people who go for it. (*Laughter*) The more people buy it, the more sure you can be it is not valid. Sincerity.

Student: Isn't sincerity a problem because we have other interests and we fool ourselves about our real interests?

Dr. Hora: Yes. We want the answer to come out our way. Yes? We want to be thought of as knowing. We are right; others are wrong. Somehow we are looking out for number one. So the human mind has become twisted from childhood on, and miseducated. And then the study of Metapsychiatry seems to be very difficult and very slow, and it is the simplest thing in the world. But who wants to be simple—see? If you are simple, then you are labeled as a simpleton. You are a simpleton. And "simpleton" means you are stupid.

Somebody not long ago wrote me a letter and asked me to write a recommendation for her to join another school. A school of psychology. So I said, "Do you realize what you are asking me to do? You are asking me to lie. You are asking me to influence people. You are asking me to deny my true thoughts about this situation, all in the name of kindness. If I do this, I would just be hurting you, because the whole thing is just influencing. You cannot ask me to influence somebody on your behalf. This is not a legal deal." She didn't realize that she was so phony and willful. She didn't stop to think about what she was doing. So I wrote to her: *Have you ever heard of self-confirmatory stupidity?* (*Laughter*) The whole thing stopped.

Student: So we really can't go through life in an undisciplined way. We really have to be vigilant all the time so that we can be aware of what we are thinking.

Dr. Hora: It depends on whether you are interested in the Truth or in winning or losing or something, cleverness, or effectiveness in influencing people to get what you want. It all depends. But if we are here for God, we cannot do these things. We cannot lie. We cannot influence.

Student: I would like to ask something. Let's say you lose your temper and you are angry, and you recognize it, you regret it, and you are interested in reorientation. What about this thought? Let's say you open one of the books or listen to a tape or something, and you are in an endeavor to reorient your thoughts, and then you have the thought, *If I have these invalid thoughts, how do I have the nerve to say that I am praying when I just had these invalid thoughts?* Do you know what I mean? You don't feel you have the right to be a representative of God's thoughts when you have just really come up out of the sea of mental garbage. I mean, wallowing in it or something like that. And you think that this is all hypocrisy. First you are angry and there is no love in your consciousness, and the next thing you are turning to God and hoping for peace or something like that.

Dr. Hora: Are we praying for a reward?

Student: I know the answer is no. But, it's almost that you think you are not worthy to participate in the good of God. That kind of thing.

Dr. Hora: In Metapsychiatry, we are learning that God is not a merit system. You don't have to deserve the grace of enlightenment. You cannot get it from God as a reward for anything.

Student: Also, it is not ourselves who are to blame in the issue. Whatever happened is to blame. It is just some invalid idea that captivated us for a time.

Dr. Hora: Self-blame is self-confirmatory. So what is your idea of prayer? You want to be forgiven because you are praying? We would be influencing God to condone our ignorance. We cannot influence God for anything.

Student: In turning aside from the sea of mental garbage, it appears that you are doing something—picking up a book or turning to a tape, or turning to something.

Dr. Hora: Do we deserve a present for it?

Student: There is a tendency then to take credit for it, because we do the turning.

Student: When we love peace. If you love peace and then you just get mad, there is no peace, so the turning is to get back into that state of consciousness because you love it. You can't stand it without peace.

Dr. Hora: Yes! Right. It has nothing to do with being forgiven or not forgiven. God is infinite mercy. You don't have to ask forgiveness. You don't have to speak three times over your left shoulder to get something. You just have to straighten out your head (*laughter*) and see life in the right context, and that in itself takes care of it. We don't have to ask forgiveness from God. God doesn't know that we are sinners. There is no sin. There is only stupidity. There is not a merit system. It is an *is* system. Ask one of our students, and she will tell you "Is you is or is you ain't," right? That is all there is to it. It is so simple, isn't it? (*Laughter*)

4

Self-Confirmatory Ideation

Student: This is just a very general question: Self-confirmation seems so big. I mean everything can be interpreted as self-confirmatory, unless we really understand God. It's difficult.

Dr. Hora: Yes.

Student: It really is difficult, because just when I think I have understood something, another opportunity comes up, and opportunities are forever knocking. I am amazed at the intensity of this desire to want to confirm myself.

Dr. Hora: Right.

Student: And especially at work there is so much opportunity with all the interaction, and sometimes I have to sit at my desk and say, "I am not leaving, because I can see an invalid motivation." I would like to understand it so that it doesn't seem like such an arduous process. How do you get beyond this? It seems like an effort.

Dr. Hora: Yes. Any comment on this problem?

Student: Well, of course, there is prayer. God-centered living is the only alternative. But it's understandable, because God-centered living is difficult.

Dr. Hora: You have this "God-centered living" from the Lord's Prayer?

Student: Yes.

Dr. Hora: The Metapsychiatric interpretation of the Lord's Prayer says, "God-centered living is the only alternative to self-confirmatory ideation." Do we all know this? So what's wrong with self-confirmatory ideation? Is there a law against it? This is a free country, right? This stinks. Has it been invented by Metapsychiatry to make your life miserable? (*Laughter*) Is it a cruel joke? What do you think?

Student: It's just that when we are involved in self-confirmation, it always brings trouble.

Dr. Hora: Are you sure this is really so?

Student: Oh, I'm sure. (*Laughter*) That's the easy part.

Student: Dr. Hora, it seems we can get into so-called "good" self-confirmation. What I mean is, the other day I was thinking of something similar. Suppose you clean up a lot of stuff in your life. Now, we've learned here that we express spiritual qualities. I was thinking of how difficult that is, though. Because if you're a father, you express fatherly qualities. Yet it is so easy to get caught in "I am a father; this is my son." Or, as you say, "We are friendly because God is love," which is a wonderful quality. But instead I *have* friends and stick to this sense of personhood. So, I was thinking that even when it comes to good qualities, I have a problem. I realize that I have heard this so many times, to "express spiritual qualities." But it's like they stick somewhere. And I feel that either I am doing it or I think I am somebody's brother or I think I am somebody's son or somebody's friend. And I don't know how to get beyond the good qualities.

Dr. Hora: Whose son are you?

Student: There is such a big difference between repeating the principles we've learned here, saying them, and paying attention to them to the point where we really think that we are praying—there is a big difference between that and suddenly breaking through so that you're not just talking about them or repeating them, but you make that transition to *being* them. It's so easy to fool yourself into thinking that when you are praying and really studying and meditating, you're doing what God requires. It's not. It's different. I don't know how to put it into words, but it's something else beyond that. I think that's what she was talking about. Breaking through. It seems like it's a wall 20 feet thick that you have to get through so you can really *be* what we are learning—so these lofty ideas are not something that we are praying about, but something that we really know and manifest.

Student: So is that what you refer to as "actualizing" spiritual principles? Is "actualizing" the right word?

Dr. Hora: Actually, the principles are actual. They reveal the nature of reality, every one of them, so they are actual. They don't need to be actualized; they need to be realized. Reality is to be realized. And when reality becomes real to us, we have a realization. Are we just playing with words here?

Student: No.

Dr. Hora: There are realized individuals, which is synonymous with being enlightened, and there are intellectually informed students of Metapsychiatry who know *about* these things. They can even quote you verbatim. But they really haven't realized it, so they don't have the benefit of it. And then there are people who are skeptical about it. Then there are those who don't know anything about it. So, first we get information, and then we have to study and seek realization, which appears as transformation. When we have realized the validity and the truth, which these principles speak about, then we are transformed. The Bible says, "[I]f any man be in Christ, he is a new creature: old things are passed away; behold, all things are become new" (2 Corinthians 5:17). How do we climb into Christ? What does this mean—if anyone is in Christ, he has undergone a transformation to the point that he is a new creature? He has new shoes, new clothes, a new hairdo? (*Laughing*) That's not enough. This transformation has to be existential. And it validates itself in a change in character, in style, in mode of being-in-the-world, and many of the vicissitudes of unenlightened life disappear. "Get thee behind me, Satan," and don't bother me no more! (*Laughing*) The inclination toward self-confirmatory thinking and behaving is the devil. It's always whispering to you, "Well, a little bragging, a little bellyaching, a little gossiping, they won't hurt you, almost everybody is doing it"—yes? The teenager who says, "But Mom, everybody is wearing these skirts," or whatever—these kinds of people have an urge to conform and to go one better. If you just conform, you get lost in the shuffle. But if you conform and go one better, then you'll become outstanding, right? Like a sore thumb! (*Laughing*) Now, one thing is very mysterious. Whenever someone yields to the temptation to think in self-confirmatory ways, with any kind of issue, essentially very often there is a self-confirmatory element somewhere in the body, and a symptom arises. There is no way of knowing where it is going to hit you. But invariably self-confirmatory ideation becomes manifest in the form of a symptom, a problem, a pain, an itch, a scratch, or an accident of some sort. Now, how does the body know that the mind is involved in self-confirmatory ideation? I listened to a lecture on the radio this afternoon about a man who wrote a book about consciousness. He said that he's an expert. He said, "Consciousness is very mysterious, but I know that it is on a material basis. But the one thing I *don't* know is how consciousness is connected with the body." He can't figure this out, but he knows that it is material, which means he doesn't know anything. If you try to understand consciousness on a material basis, you don't get anywhere. Now, some of you have experienced healings of certain physical symptoms and the connection between the symptom and the self-confirmatory ideation is not clear. "Why

should I get a neck ache or an earache or something if I am thinking about how wonderful I am, or something like that?" People
don't understand how their body selects the symptom to go with
the self-confirmatory thought. Did you ever think of this? Jimmy
Durante had the answer. What was his answer?

Student: "The nose knows."

Dr. Hora: "The nose knows." (*Laughing*) And so we can say the body
seems to know our innermost secret thoughts. The body speaks,
and a student of Metapsychiatry learns to understand what the
body is saying. And it is always saying the same thing: "You are
bragging, you are bellyaching, you are bullying, you are bullshit-
ting, you are bickering." Right? That is what the body keeps
saying, yes? "You're a lot of baloney." The body always tells us
this. And if we learn to listen to what our body says, we discover
the remedy to the problem. The remedy is always this: Abandon
self-confirmatory ideation and turn your attention to the truth of
your being. And when you become more interested in the truth of
your being than in self-confirmatory ideation, you are released
from the consequences of self-confirmatory ideation.

Student: Can you explain it any more than to say that the body seems
to know?

Dr. Hora: What more do you want?

Student: I don't know. The body seems to know. How does the body
know? I know that it seems to know. How does it know?

Dr. Hora: How does the body know? Well, as I said, the body is a
language that can translate human thoughts into physical symptoms. It's like a computer, when you have something on the screen
and you can press a button and the printer will know what is on
the screen and print it out. Yes? Suppose you have a migraine
headache—how does the head know what the mind is thinking?

Or if you get a charley horse in your leg, how does the leg know what you are dreaming about, what your thoughts are? So the body and the mind, the human mind, are one; it's one phenomenon.

Student: Isn't there also something associated with the repression of the thought? For instance, if you have an angry thought and you're fully aware of that angry thought, it doesn't as quickly express itself as a physical symptom. It's the repression of it that seems to result in the appearance of the symptom in the body.

Dr. Hora: You're right. Of course. It's called somatization. If we have learned to be conscious of what we are thinking day and night, then physical symptoms will be less likely to occur. The thought doesn't have to hit us over the head; we already are aware of it. It's very helpful, through training in meditation, to develop the faculty of conscious awareness of our thoughts day and night, whether asleep or awake. If we have learned this, we will be spared physical symptoms. And physical symptoms are very dangerous. What is the danger in physical symptoms?

Student: They lead you further and further away from God and closer and closer to the material man. And then you're lost.

Dr. Hora: Yes, that's right.

Student: I had an interesting thing happen. I had had a physical symptom for a very long time that was healed and was fine. And I had a little bit of backsliding—thoughts that I had had all my life that were invalid—and right in that spot, even though there is nothing there anymore, I got a pain. And I told Dr. Hora, and he said, "The body remembers." And that is the reason that I asked the question. Obviously the body remembers. It just couldn't be that you get this pain in this particular spot. How did the body remember?

Dr. Hora: You have a very talented body. (*Laughter*)

Student: Asking how the body knows seems a little bit like a trick question. Because it attributes a power to the body that really doesn't exist. We know that the body is simply a manifestation of thought. It's the thought that's the issue, not the body.

Dr. Hora: You're absolutely right. Yes. But this trick question is helpful. We'll tolerate a trick.

Student: I wasn't being critical. (*Laughter*)

Dr. Hora: OK, so she is complaining, "Why can't I indulge myself in the office and show off and confirm myself as this wonderful person, which I really am?" (*Laughter*)

Student: Maybe I'm not. (*Laughter*)

Dr. Hora: Isn't it cruel that Metapsychiatry deprives us of the pleasure of self-confirmatory behavior? Well it would seem like it's a great sacrifice, turning attention away from self. When we turn our attention away from self but not toward God, where are we? The Bible says you're nowhere.

Student: That's comforting. (*Laughter*)

Dr. Hora: Selfhood apart from God is an illusion. So if you are confirming yourself, you are nowhere. You're in an illusion; you *are* an illusion, and you are not in touch with Reality. It is dangerous to be out of touch with Reality. On the other hand, we can feel, "Look it would feel so good if I could show off a little with my new dress, my hairdo, how beautiful I am, how dry I am." (*Laughter*) We are constantly being tempted. It's a universal inclination in humans to confirm themselves, to entertain self-confirmatory ideas. Now, this is a no-no. So if we cannot confirm ourselves, what do we do? Well, the Bible says you have to commit yourself to God. Commit thy thoughts, thy motivations, thine interests, every thought. Everything concerning yourself has to be focused on the good of God. To that end, we have a gyroscope. Have you ever seen a gyroscope? No? What is a gyroscope? Does anybody know?

Student: It's an instrument to steer you correctly. In other words, if you are off on the wrong angle or direction, it shows you, and it—

Dr. Hora: —automatically steers your boat (or plane, if you're a flier) in the right direction. Before you start out, you set it at a certain angle according to the compass, and then it's instrumental. It's like an autopilot. A gyroscope will keep your boat always moving in that set direction.

Student: And that's why we have you, Dr. Hora?

Dr. Hora: I am not a gyroscope. (*Laughter*)

Student: But it seems that you are.

Dr. Hora: I am just a builder of gyroscopes. I build them. The First Principle of Metapsychiatry is the gyroscope for us. How does the First Principle maintain us in moving in the right direction? How does it work?

Student: It keeps our interest focused. The First Principle keeps our interest focused. And if we notice that we are off track, we turn.

Dr. Hora: If the self-confirmatory winds are blowing, they keep dislodging us, turning our interest toward self and toward others. The winds and the currents in life keep on pushing our interest in the direction of self and others. The gyroscope keeps bringing us back to the interest in the good of God, which is spiritual blessedness. Now the question is, what do you appreciate more, bragging or spiritual blessedness? What do you think?

Student: Even after we see time and time again the fruits of spiritual blessedness, there is still always a strong temptation. It seems so hard to understand that even after we have seen it so many times, we don't fully appreciate it all the time.

Dr. Hora: In our culture and society there are all kinds of pressures and seductive influences. These are the winds. And everything from television and the media and society, parties, and such, shifts the direction of our interest into the sphere of interaction thinking and self-confirmatory ideation. And that's what the world consists of. Jesus said that you have to overcome the world. We have to overcome self-confirmatory ideation. And that's the value of the gyroscope in life. It's a spiritual gyroscope.

Student: I am trying to break down self-confirmatory ideation. It's so funny. Does one need to realize the doubt that this self, which seems so important, actually exists?

Dr. Hora: Well, if you have a doubt, then you may agonize over it. As long as we doubt something, we're agonizing: Is it or ain't it? "Is you is, or is you ain't?"

Student: It seems to me so natural to think that I'm a self, so I thought if I doubt that, then perhaps I might find out: What am I if I am not that?

Dr. Hora: This kind of speculation comes later. The first thing to learn is that self-confirmation is self-destruction, and self-destruction is self-confirmation. Once you can *clearly* see that this is so, then you begin to lose interest in this kind of sense of self. And then your question becomes clearer. You cannot start out by just saying, "There is no self. Hora says so. But I am not sure; maybe there is, somewhere," or something like that. No, the best way to understand this problem is to experience the pain and the consequences of self-confirmatory ideation. When you have had several painful experiences, you can see the connection, right? Then you already understand that here is something that appears to be completely human and normal—even desirable—and it is an enemy. It is dangerous and harmful and inevitably leads us to suffering. Once you can see that there is a direct connection between our problems and this type of thinking, you can say, "Well, where do I go from here? How is this possible? Is it so bad to think that I am pretty or that I am smart or I am better than the next guy?" There are a million ways you can entertain self-confirmatory ideas, and invariably you run into trouble with that. Once you understand it, you have seen it; you have experienced it; it's no theory; it's not intellectual information. And you taste the bitter fruits of that kind of thinking; then you say, "Well, this is not worth it." Right? "I'd better go to Kelcy's and get a drink."

Student: What is Kelcy's?

Dr. Hora: (*Laughter*) It's the corner—

Student: —tavern in *All in the Family*—Archie Bunker's. (*Laughter*)

Dr. Hora: Archie Bunker's. Many people, when they come to this dilemma, recognizing that they are hurting, try to find another solution, either through drugs or through alcohol or through sex or through fighting—or a million ways of avoiding the issue and getting deeper into trouble. If you try to avoid the issue, you get deeper into trouble.

Student: You find stuff all the time that is self-confirmatory, to the point where you say, "I can't stand myself!" You can't stand the fact that you're so involved!

Dr. Hora: So you find a solution. Most people find their own solution. There is only one right solution: Commit thy ways, thy thoughts, unto the Lord, and thou shalt be established. We are here to manifest the perfection of God's being. This is our purpose in the world: to manifest the perfection of God's being. And when we appreciate this truth, then self-confirmatory ideation fades away from our thoughts and we find ourselves in the land of PAGL. Do you know where that is? Have you ever visited this land? In the land of PAGL, there is peace, assurance, gratitude, love, freedom, wisdom, joy, and healing. It's a fringe benefit.

Student: Dr. Hora, if all that we know is self-referential...I've come to discover how I turn everything into how it's affecting *me*. So that, I know very well.

Dr. Hora: OK.

Student: OK. How then can you go from that to God-confirmatory or God-referential thinking, let's say, when you really don't know anything about God? I mean, I can see the mistake of self-referential thinking; it's clearly a problem. I can meditate on these ideas, but how can I possibly know God?

Dr. Hora: It's interesting; this student has changed a word. Have you noticed?

Student: "Self-referential."

Dr. Hora: She changed a word. It sounds like she is talking about the same thing—let's not be picayune—but what happens when we accept this word "self-referential"?

Student: It sounds more acceptable in a way. If we say that, then the idea of self-confirmation kind of loses its power.

Dr. Hora: Of course. Of course, because the important word is "confirmation." "Self-referential" means "I am referring to something that is not immediately connected with me." There are reference libraries where we can refer to this or that, and we can refer to God, but when we speak about self-confirmation, we speak about something that is not a *reference* to the self but that is the *confirmation* of the *reality* of the self. So when you engage in self-confirmatory ideation, it is entirely different from self-referential thinking, because it says something else. The self-confirmatory thought says, *I am a person in a body, a physical entity entirely apart from God.* When you refer to "self-referential," you are talking about a book, or about another thing, referring to yourself. That is not the same as confirming yourself. And if you confirm yourself, and this self, which you have confirmed as real, gets you into trouble, then it immediately helps you to be aware that you have hurt yourself.

Now, what is the meaning of, after 45 minutes of talking about self-confirmatory ideation and writing 15 books about it, here comes a student who changes the wording into something that is less than the other word? The urge is to confirm the reality of the self. If we say "self-referential," we tend to think about something that is not necessarily something of importance. Every time somebody entertains a self-confirmatory thought, he says, "I am a physical person." And when you do that, you discover yourself as a liar. You're lying. You're confirming something that seems to be but isn't. Now, if somebody alters this term, he is trying to avoid facing this lie. He says, "I am not talking about the lie, I am *referring* to something not very intimately related to my existential reality." When we go to a reference library, referring to a book somewhere on the shelf, that's a reference library; we don't have to seek a confirmatory book—unless you are looking for a Metapsychiatric book (*laughing*). There's always this tendency for people to sort of trivialize the technical terms that we use. For instance, every time I ask somebody, "Can you remember the definition of perfect love?"—what do we hear, what do they say?

Student: Nonconditional—

Dr. Hora: Immediately, forget about the nonpersonal and start with the nonconditional. What are they doing? They are trying to make it easier for themselves (*laughing*). But what do you get if you make it easier for yourself? Then why bother? (*Laughing*) Then you will just be satisfied with knowing intellectually about something that you read. So we're not nitpicking about the precision of our words. Words must be precisely used; otherwise, we deprive ourselves of the benefit of understanding.

Student: Well, I was not throwing out the word "self-confirmation." What I have been struggling with is the issue of personalism. So, it occurred to me that, because I have trouble with that word, "personalism"—to really understand, because it's such a part of me that it was difficult to see it or separate it.

Dr. Hora: Can you tell us the definition of "personalism?"

Student: Well, no, I can't tell you the definition—

Dr. Hora: No?

Student: —but I would like to just say that what occurred to me is "self-referential thinking"—that somehow that word came to me to help me see how I personalize everything.

Dr. Hora: Send it back. It came to you; send it back. (*Laughter*)

Student: Really? It's so helpful!

Dr. Hora: Who knows the definition of "personalism"? What is personalism? Nobody knows? Can't remember?

Student: Well, I guess it's the idea that we're independent physical entities with minds of our own.

Student: Thinking about what others are thinking about what you're thinking about?

Dr. Hora: Right. Exactly. Thinking about what others are thinking about what we are thinking. This is personalism. Now, what's wrong with that? (*Laughter*) Isn't that very sociable, friendly?

Student: I think that the main thing that's wrong with it is that it leads to insanity. (*Laughter*)

Dr. Hora: Yes, of course. If you have ever spoken to someone who was deranged, you will always hear him say, "That thing that I..." and, "I am this, and them," and everything they say is about persons thinking about this person and involved in a personal relationship. "Self and other" is the essence of their thinking, and they cannot see beyond self and other. How is it possible that there could be reality that is beyond the relationship between self and others? What else is there? The desk itself? (*Laughter*) We have to transcend this limited perspective on reality. That's why Jesus said to be of good cheer, that there is a way to overcome the world.

Student: Dr. Hora, I was assuming I understood the word "ideation." I am not sure that I understand it correctly. So, what is the definition of "ideation"?

Dr. Hora: Can someone help us?

Student: It's been described as focused thinking on a specific area, a tendency to think about something.

Dr. Hora: Yes, it's a preoccupation with ideas, any kinds of ideas. If you are preoccupied with ideas about yourself, then you are engaged in self-confirmatory ideation. You know that is a fancy word for thinking. (*Laughter*) But when we say "thinking," the implication is that we are *doing* the thoughts. Nobody can *do* a thought. But if we say "ideation," we are saying, "Certain ideas have obtained in consciousness, and we are preoccupied with these ideas." And so we cannot say, "Very well; I am engaged in self-confirmatory thinking." It would indicate that you made it up. Nobody produces thoughts in his or her brain. But if you say, "I'm involved with self-confirmatory ideation," it means that a certain idea about myself is present in consciousness, and I am messing around with it, and if I do that, there is a price to be paid. Ideation may be very strange to some people. On Saturday I spoke to an executive from a major corporation who was not a very well-educated man, but he has started reading some of the books on Metapsychiatry. He said, "I told my wife that I have learned a big word: 'self-confirmatory ideation.'" And his wife said, "What in the world is that?" Yes, it's a startling word, but we can grow to appreciate it. Then we carefully consider the implications and the consequences of unknowingly being involved in that kind of mental practice.

5

Job Fulfillment

Student: I have a question about my job. I have been at this job for about seven months. I found when I first started that it was interesting because there was a process that I had to learn. But now that I have learned it, it's sort of repetitive. It doesn't seem like there is any opportunity to learn more. What I was doing before this job was paying less but had more potential for learning and growth. I would like to know how to look at this situation, to see it more clearly.

Dr. Hora: Does anyone have an idea of how to help? Did you discuss this with your father?

Student: A little bit.

Dr. Hora: What did he say?

Student: One idea we thought about was that I could work at this other job and work for my father's company part-time, in the evening. That was one idea. It seems that what I am doing in the daytime involves no learning apart from learning the initial system process. It is repeated again and again. It does not seem to allow for my own learning.

Dr. Hora: As you know, whenever we are faced with a problem in life, we have learned to approach it with two intelligent questions. Did you do that?

Student: I think I did when I found myself being discouraged that I wasn't learning things. I said to myself, "Well, the issue is to pay attention and just do the work." But I guess I didn't ask the meaning of my experience in a more comprehensive way, like "What is the meaning of my being at this job to begin with?"

Dr. Hora: OK, so you are just like most students of Metapsychiatry. They prefer to forget to ask the right question and just suffer along without it. But if we are sincere and we would really like to be healed of a situation, we ask, "What is the meaning of my experience in this situation?" Would you like to know? (*Laughter*) Did you hear the hesitation? (*Laughter*) Some people will be stuck in a situation and unhappy and bored, but they do not touch the saving question with a 10-foot pole. They just go on suffering.

Student: We have talked about the monks carrying water and chopping wood. That is a repetitive task, but their motivation was right.

Dr. Hora: What is their motivation?

Student: They don't use the same words that we use, but they were "here for God."

Dr. Hora: They are not using the same words, but—

Student: I don't know if the monks would say they are "here for God." That seems to be the issue there.

Dr. Hora: No. The monks just said, "We are very happy." They find it a marvelous job to do this day after day, year after year, chopping wood and carrying water. They don't even have to know math or computers or anything. How can anybody be happy doing this manual labor constantly? What makes them so happy?

Student: They don't want much.

Dr. Hora: They don't want much? Are they stupid or something?

Student: That is not in their attitude.

Dr. Hora: How do you explain that?

Student: I wish I knew.

Dr. Hora: What is the meaning of discontent in a job? It is either not enough money or—

Student: Jealousy.

Dr. Hora: Jealousy?

Student: No ego gratification.

Dr. Hora: No ego gratification. What is that? What is ego gratification? He is talking about learning. It would seem that he wants a job where he could learn something, right? What do you want to learn?

Student: It seems it would be good to have skills.

Dr. Hora: Skills—oh, yes, very good.

Student: There is a skill to this job, and I was trained to do it, but now that I know it somewhat, there is no more to learn—maybe on one level. There is more than one level.

Dr. Hora: Which level is that?

Student: The level of what to do to make the process work.

Dr. Hora: Well, it is good to learn, but the question is, what lesson do we have to learn? Everybody has to learn some different lesson. Just because we are a computer specialist doesn't necessarily mean that if we learn more computer knowledge, then that will lead to our fulfillment. Being a better computer programmer is not necessarily fulfilling, right? So the question is, what is good to learn? We have to learn not only skills, but also life. What does it mean to "learn life"? Is there life after computers?

Student: Learning PAGL.

Dr. Hora: Learning PAGL. What is that?

Student: Learning what real life is.

Dr. Hora: Could you explain?

Student: Perhaps a life of spiritual values, and understanding spiritual values and principles.

Dr. Hora: What do you think of that? Isn't that very boring? Perhaps even more than your job? (*Laughter*) He speaks of learning. Most people would say there is no fun in this job, right? Did you try bringing your radio to your job? There are people who go to their jobs and listen to the radio, and there are many radios in a room competing with each other, because in our culture there is a belief that entertainment is the good life, right? The good life consists of continuous entertainment. Some people believe the good life consists of promotion, being promoted more and more and learning more, greater complicated tasks to perform, and gaining recognition and such. These are very good things, but they are not life. They are performance and concerned with feeling good and feeling more and more important, and perhaps gaining admiration plus more money. All these are cultural phenomena. Our culture fosters these ideas. We call this progress, but nobody is really ever satisfied on the job. There is no such thing as job satisfaction. Did you know that?

Student: Some people seem to perform their job with a lot of love. It is almost a hobby or avocation that they are involved in, and they are getting paid for it. I have seen this with musicians. People who work around flowers also seem to love what they are doing.

Dr. Hora: That is a good point. What is their secret? What does it take to have job satisfaction? To become a florist? You could try. It may not work for you, right? There must be more to life than jobs. There is more to life than entertainment. There is more to life than personal recognition. There is more to life than money. Who would believe that? One can ask, "What is more to life than all these things?" What are we talking about? What is life? Have you ever seen life walking?

Student: Like the expression of qualities, abundant expression of qualities.

Dr. Hora: Okay, so Coca-Cola expresses lots of fizz and qualities. That is not enough.

Student: Being here for God and expressing qualities.

Dr. Hora: Being here for God. The question was, what is life? I'll tell you a secret. Life is God. Life is God, and the issue of life is God. What are we saying when we say that? The issue of life is God. It is not self-esteem. It is not personal power. It is not entertainment. It is not recognition. It is none of those ancillary, marginal aspects of human experience. Life is God. The issue of life is God. How can we say that? What are we saying?

Student: The issue of life is God for the musician when the musician sees the beauty and the harmony in the music. For the florist, it's when the florist sees the life and the beauty and the intelligence and the balance—all of these intangible qualities—being expressed.

Dr. Hora: In other words, they are seeing God.

Student: Transcending the work they are doing.

Dr. Hora: They are involved with God, even if they are atheists. They don't have to go to church or be theologians. But if there is an appreciation of beauty, harmony, joy, gratitude, freedom, wisdom, then we are involved with life. We are looking and seeing life, which is God. Then there is no frustration, discontent, fear, anxiety, jealousy, rivalry this way and that way, and there is happiness and there is health. These people have a hobby, and they do what they enjoy. Sure, but what is the secret? The secret is that they are involved with life.

Student: It seems as if there are certain vocations that provide more of an opportunity to see these qualities of life. In other words, it seems that what you are saying is that our purpose is to come to know God, to know life. To come to know God, that is what we are here for. A student talks about certain musicians seeing these qualities. That's clear. The florists somehow see spiritual qualities in what they are seeing. It does seem as if these guys carrying water and chopping wood are able to see these same qualities. I guess that is the difficulty, that some of us have a problem seeing the spiritual qualities in the nature of the work that we are doing. Maybe sitting in front of a computer screen, he has a problem seeing the spiritual values in the task that he is performing.

Dr. Hora: Yes. Some musicians have the same problem as the computer specialists, and some florists only see the price tag, right? And they, too, have a problem. Is there a place where God is not present—for instance, let's say, in a coal mine? Suppose you are working in a coal mine. Is this a hopeless situation? Is there no God in a coal mine? There is sometimes more of God in a coal mine than on Fifth Avenue in New York. Where is God located? In consciousness. As Jesus said, "Blessed are they that hunger and thirst after the right thing, for they shall be fulfilled" (Matthew 5:6). Now, this student has a distinct experience of an unfulfilling job. He is aware of not finding fulfillment in his job assignment. Suppose tomorrow he is promoted to chief computer consultant and everybody looks at him. Will that give him fulfillment? No, just a temporary uplift. So it is with everything.

Student: So where is this issue of learning? It seems to be very important. Or is it a way of disguising the real issue?

Dr. Hora: Most people don't know what is really important. Sure, it's important to know how to program a computer and to have marketable skills, but how many people are really satisfied with their life, with their activities, with their conditions? And another thing: Suppose we sympathize with this student's position—that his particular assignment at this job is boring, unsatisfactory, and is not taking into consideration his potential as a computer specialist. Then it is legitimate for him to ask, "How could I be set free of my limitations on this job?" Well, psychologists or occupational therapists would say, "Go to the supervisor and talk to him and tell him how you feel." You could try that. You might even succeed to some extent, but it may not be enough. The Bible says promotion cometh from above. Jesus said, "All power is given unto me from above."[5] What would you do with this?

Student: It is not my job to be concerned about the specifics of where I am working or what I am doing or what I am learning—just to do what is in front of me, and it is up to God to take control.

Dr. Hora: Do you understand us to say you have to be reconciled to your situation? That is what Mother Teresa said to the lepers in India: "Be glad that you have this affliction. It is a sign of a special love from God. Reconcile yourself to this condition." That is not very helpful, right? Then you will not even pray for a healing. We are not saying you must reconcile yourself to this unsatisfactory job situation—no. The question is, what would be most helpful in healing the discontent that he is experiencing? That is the issue, isn't it? How can we be healed of discontent?

---

[5] "And Jesus came and spake unto them, saying, All power is given unto me in heaven and in earth" (Matthew 28:18).

Student: We have to understand what that discontentment is, because obviously there is an invalid motivation. If at work we are discontented, we have to look at our motivation, understand it, and seek to understand God in that situation. So when you say that we have to live life by seeking God in every situation, the discontentment needs to be seen. And now we need to replace it with valid motivation, which is that we work for God. There is obviously something at this job for the student to learn—to see God—and then the limitation would be lifted because he would be free.

Dr. Hora: Do we all understand this? She knows.

Student: I am not sure I get it yet. If the student is discontented, the basis for the discontent has to be something that he wants or doesn't want.

Dr. Hora: Right.

Student: So we start from there. That's where our problems start, with something we want or don't want. So he wants a job that has more excitement, or more interest or whatever you want to say. He doesn't want this kind of a job.

Dr. Hora: You want a challenging job?

Student: It seems as if we are saying that we need to reconcile ourselves to what we have.

Dr. Hora: That may seem to you to be what was said, but nobody said that.

Student: I understand that can't be right. I know it can't be right.

Dr. Hora: No. We don't lie down and die. We die standing up. (*Laughter*)

Student: Clearly paying attention to being here for God is different from reconciling oneself.

Dr. Hora: Exactly. Now what does it mean to be here for God?

Student: To be issue-oriented.

Dr. Hora: That's correct. Now could you explain what that means? The issue of life is God, and if we are interested in fulfillment and living a life of fulfillment, we have to find the answer to this problem.

Student: It seems to me the main issue is usefulness. So we look to maximize our usefulness by seeking in the situation to understand the need as best we can, and by looking for the right values. Looking for God in the job is looking for those existentially valid values that are part of the work that he has to do. In my experience, by attempting to be useful, by seeking to be useful, new opportunities always seem to arise.

Dr. Hora: That is a very important point. OK, but he says, "I am fully useful, but this job limits my usefulness because I don't have the opportunity to express more of my potential. So I feel legitimately discontented, because my potential is not given the opportunity to express itself in this lousy job." (*Laughter*) He could then jump up and say, "Take this job and shove it." (*Laughter*)

The interesting thing is that Jesus, as a counselor for unemployed people, didn't say, "You have to find how to improve, how to become more fulfilled in your job. If you are unhappy in computers, your tendency is to somehow find in computer work something more that will fulfill you—a better computer, a new computer or something. We always try to improve our material foundation for fulfillment. If in the material world we are unfulfilled, we want to find the solution to this in the *material* world—a better job, a better assignment, higher pay. It is natural to think this way, but Jesus didn't say, "If you are not satisfied, then improve your material situation." On the contrary, he said that if you want fulfillment, you have to hunger and thirst after right understanding, not of the computer sciences but of life itself. It is interesting. You would say, "What are you talking about? This has no relevancy to my job, to hunger and thirst after right understanding of life." But what he said is that if you hunger and thirst after right understanding of life, you will find fulfillment. Logically this doesn't make any sense, because it doesn't seem to be related to the source of discontent. It is very strange. How can our hunger and thirst after the right understanding of life lead to a better job as a computer specialist?

Student: God is life. So the right understanding of God somehow makes everything else work out better. Somehow, right understanding heals everything.

Dr. Hora: So now what we do is we start praying. How do we pray? How would he have to pray about being healed of this discontent so that he would be led to discover fulfillment?

Student: A good start might be the four "Ws."

Dr. Hora: Yes; in what way will that lead to fulfillment?

Student: If he could begin to understand who he is, what he is, where he is, and what his purpose is, that would lead him into a spiritual mode from a material mode. It would open up the channel to ideas from God that is available to us. It would make available to him inspired ideas without prejudging what should be or shouldn't be, and opportunities and new challenges would become available.

Dr. Hora: Isn't that wonderful? This is a total conversion. (*Laughter*)

Student: I can't wait to listen to this tape. (*Laughter*)

Dr. Hora: That is exactly true. When we seek to understand life as God, everything opens up, and we can be flooded with Divinely authorized new ideas and new possibilities, and just what is needed can come about. It's an unfolding of our situation where we get healed of discontent and we find that we are being active. We are in the right place at the right time in the right way and doing the right work for which God has given us certain talents. How can we say, "the right place, the right time, the right work, the right way"? How can we make such a statement? Simply because God is infinite perfection. God's reality is absolutely perfect, and within this perfect universe we are perfect creations of God. And if everything is perfect and we are perfect, then everything in our lives becomes perfect. That includes the job and good-looking girls. (*Laughter*) Everything becomes possible. As it is written in the Bible, "Be ye therefore perfect, even as your Father...in heaven is perfect" (Matthew 5:48). The perfection of reality unfolds itself before us, around us, and within us, and that's a perfect healing. Next time you want to know something, ask *her*. (*Laughter*) That was nice.

Student: Dr. Hora, a couple of years ago this question came up, and I think you brought up a verse that was helpful, too. I don't know exactly how it goes, something like "If you have been faithful first in small things and you become perfect to the maximum, inevitably something has to work."

Dr. Hora: Well, you can approach it slowly or faster. One way to practice perfection is by remembering what perfect love is. Anyone who endeavors to love perfectly in his daily life will discover God's perfect universe. It is sort of a latchkey into paradise. If we practice perfect love, we cannot fail to enter into the realm of Divine perfection. Do we know what perfect love is?

Student: It's God's love for us.

Dr. Hora: That's perfect, but what about us? We have to express perfect love. How do we do that?

Student: Nonpersonal, nonconditional—

Dr. Hora: Nonpersonal, nonconditional benevolence. If we practice it in daily life, it will bring us closer and closer into that dimension that is called Divine Reality, which is perfect.

Student: People often say, "What I am really looking for is to be more expansive or to be more expressive." Is there such a thing as divine discontent, or are people just saying that?

Dr. Hora: In poetry you can find it, yes. Some poets use that phrase, but that phrase is not legitimate, because it can be easily misunderstood as meaning that God is discontented. How could God be discontented if He is perfect? There is no such thing, really. We can experience discontent in the human experience. In the human condition, there is a lot of discontent. But we seek to be redeemed from this condition and raised up to the level of spiritual perfection that is our birthright. We are meant to be perfect in every way.

Student: So if one has a job experience of not feeling as if one's talents are being utilized, what is the meaning of that?

Dr. Hora: Where were you tonight? (*Laughter*)

Student: I look back over the years and I find that I have been in jobs that are beneath me. I never have been called upon to exercise what I think I am capable of.

Dr. Hora: Your full potential.

Student: So I have must have been pursuing some invalid ideas. I don't know what it is. It has not gone away, and this has kind of limited the potential that otherwise might have evolved. So I am a failure.

Dr. Hora: Congratulations. (*Laughter*)

Student: It sounds like the ego has a big problem. You spoke before about the coal mine, that you could have just as much of God there as on Fifth Avenue, or more. It must be because we don't know perfect love, because we feel somebody has to see our love; we have to have objects, and we must exist on a larger scale. You are telling us it can be expressed anywhere and nobody has to be around to see it, and we can get spiritual fulfillment from that moment. I guess it is so ingrained for us to want to give it *to* somebody, or have an audience.

Dr. Hora: You could even charge for it. (*Laughter*) Is there such a thing as success and failure in Divine Reality? We know on the human plane, in the human experience, there is a lot of success and failure. But in Divine Reality, could there be failure? Was Jesus successful, or was he a failure? There are people who point at the Crucifixion as the proof of the failure of the man and the failure of his teachings and of his career.

Student: Then there was the Resurrection a few days later.

Dr. Hora: Do you believe in the Resurrection?

Student: Yes!

Dr. Hora: Believing doesn't help. (*Laughter*)

Student: You set me up. (*Laughter*)

Dr. Hora: The whole history of Christianity keeps stumbling over the word "belief." It doesn't do anything for you if you believe or if you disbelieve. Most good Christians are brought up to think this way—even the Bible speaks about believing. "Believe, believe, believe." It is very easy to believe. All you have to do is to doubt, and you will believe. But the doubt never goes away; therefore, your belief is of no value. Only understanding can stand by itself. Believing cannot exist without disbelieving. It's a tragic dualism. So if somebody is encouraging you to just believe, and believe in Jesus Christ, to have a personal relationship with him, etc., it doesn't get you anywhere.

Student: You are talking about certain people saying his life was a failure because he went through the Crucifixion. But then you could say that there was a Resurrection, so his life was successful. I don't know.

Dr. Hora: Usually you are asked to believe that the Crucifixion and the Resurrection really happened. How can you know? You cannot know. So you can say, "I believe. I believe that it really happened." So where does that get you? You can be accepted in the church, but it doesn't get you anywhere.

Student: It doesn't make any difference.

Dr. Hora: No, of course. There is only one possibility in the face of this issue, and that is if we understand the meaning of crucifixion and the meaning of resurrection (John 19:1-37). If we understand these things, then we don't have to believe. Nobody can sell it to us, and we don't have to buy it. We look at it and we know what the meaning of these stories and claims is. Now, anybody who would like to understand the Crucifixion and the Resurrection in such a way that you wouldn't have to believe or disbelieve is well advised to read a little pamphlet—*Commentaries on Scripture.* Once you understand the meaning of these symbolic events, then you can say, "Well, of course we don't have to believe it or argue about it, did it happen or didn't it happen...I know it makes a lot of sense, and it is beautiful." It is very helpful if we understand it. No more arguing whether it was or it wasn't, to believe or not believe. All these things disappear, and you find peace. You don't have to agonize over it.

Student: But you did ask the question "Is there failure in Divine Reality?"

Dr. Hora: Yes, thank you for reminding me. If you don't understand the Crucifixion and the Resurrection, then you naturally will have a tendency to think that this guy is a failure. Look what happened to him. Here is a man of God, a fantastic phenomenon in the history of mankind, and he is a failure. They killed him, finished. If you try to believe that it happened, you will never know. You will just believe the rest of your life, and you will always doubt. But if you understand the meaning, then you won't have to believe. You will be at peace. It's all right. It is meaningful, fantastically meaningful. Jesus did everything at every step of the way. He had one motivation: to explain God to the world. He did it all the way to the end, and the Crucifixion and the Resurrection are just another way to explain God. And if you read the booklet, you will know.

6

Loneliness and Wanting

Student: Last week we ended the group talking about the idea of loneliness. I don't really understand what loneliness is other than when I have a sense of anxiety for no particular reason. It seems that is loneliness. So in addressing that anxiety, there are two things one can do—either do something to change focus or pray or meditate, or do something that has to be done. There are a variety of choices, but I am not really clear on the dynamics, because there are so many distractions. There are so many things we need to take care of. So the anxiety kind of continues. It is like a fleeting thing. It comes and goes. It is very easy to do something to forget about it, because it is not that major. There are enough things to distract us that are not harmful to us. It is not a major event. Yet I see the significance and the importance of being healed of loneliness. It is not really clear enough for me to work with it. I just know it exists.

Dr. Hora: Who can help us solve this mystery of loneliness? Has anybody ever been lonely?

Student: Maybe part of what she is bringing up is, does loneliness depend on the presence or absence of other individuals?

Dr. Hora: Usually that is how it appears to be, doesn't it? It is a desire for companionship. It is a psychological explanation. It meets the eye right away. When we are lonely, we want somebody to come and cheer us up, right?

Student: But if you don't turn to somebody else...I mean, you can turn to activities so that you don't use someone to fill that void.

Dr. Hora: You can get yourself distracted with something—like playing with cards, solitaire. It is either companionship or activity. What else?

Student: It doesn't always have to be an individual.

Dr. Hora: So it is either companionship or activity. What else?

Student: The anxiety isn't always loneliness, is it?

Dr. Hora: Anxiety is anxiety. Loneliness is loneliness.

Student: I thought she said that the anxiety meant that she was lonely, and I thought that anxiety could have many meanings. Maybe I misunderstood.

Dr. Hora: What did you misunderstand?

Student: I said that it seems that there is this anxiety, just like a current. No major concern, but it seems like an anxiety to do something so as not to feel lonely.

Dr. Hora: To alleviate this unpleasant sensation of considering ourselves lonely.

Student: Yes, to some extent—it is anxiety, but it is not.

Dr. Hora: What does loneliness have in common with anxiety?

Student: We don't want to feel lonely.

Dr. Hora: We don't *want* to feel lonely, and that creates anxiety. The common denominator between anxiety and loneliness is that in both instances we want something. We want something to distract us from our thoughts about being alone, unloved, unrequited. (*Laughter*)

There are many solutions to this problem. You can go to a bar and get drunk. You can pick a fight with your friends and have an exciting time. You can join a hate group and have your head shaved off. What do they call these guys? Skinheads. You can do that, right? Or you can meet a girl or a boy and go out on a date and get into a fight later. (*Laughter*) You see, most people, when they are in distress of some kind—and loneliness is distress, anxiety is distress—the first thing we think about is, *What will make me feel better?* Yes?

If that is your thought, you are lost. Because "feeling better" isn't going to heal the problem. We think, *All I want is a cigarette. Get me a smoke or something.* Most people deal with these stressful experiences by looking for some way of alleviating the distress, and you can go from one thing to another endlessly. It isn't going to get healed. You can find temporary relief, yes? Like Anacin, fast, fast relief…but that is not a healing. A healing is a much greater issue.

What is the issue with healing? Regulate the temperature? (*Laughter*) That is a remedy, too. Usually when we have stress of some kind, the human approach is to find fast relief. If you are satisfied with that, OK. There is no law against it. Drug addiction is just a search for fast relief. People are in very uncomfortable situations, and a drug can alleviate the distress temporarily, but it is not a solution. Similarly, if we have a headache, we take an aspirin or [other] drugs, which are freely available. Anybody can reach out and find something that would relieve his or her distress.

Now, suppose you are a bunch of crazy people who say, "I am not going to look for fast relief; I would like to be healed of the inclination toward this problem." Once you have this higher viewpoint, you rise above the human level to a higher level of intelligence, and you ask a question: *What could heal me from the inclination towards being a human person?* Well, you become a dog, learn to bark! (*Laughter*)

We are not looking for fast relief. It takes courage and wisdom. Then we start asking a different question. Not "How can I get relief?" but "What is the meaning of the inclination toward these experiences?" When we sincerely are interested in understanding the meaning, God provides the answer. What does God have to say?

Student: You said before that it is that you want something.

Dr. Hora: It is perfectly legitimate to want something, isn't it?

Student: It is legitimate, but it would never get you out of any trouble.

Dr. Hora: It is not legitimate to want anything. Would you believe that?

Student: It is not legitimate because it keeps us on a human level of thinking?

Dr. Hora: Yes. The Bible says, God has created us perfect in his own image and likeness (Genesis 1:26, 27), and it says, "Be ye therefore perfect, even as your Father…in heaven is perfect" (Matthew 5:48). So will this heal us? Will this be the solution? It could, if we are sincere enough and have come to understand the reality of God as the basic power of life and love in the universe. Then we can meditate about the perfection of Divine creation and our place in it, and we can perhaps become aware of the fact that we don't have to crave what we want. Wanting is the problem, always, no matter what the problem is. It can be a million kinds of things of different intensity and gravity and fear. The problem is always in a belief that it is legitimate for us to want. Who would believe that it is not legitimate for us to want? Everybody wants something.

Isn't that what you hear? Nobody is perfect. Isn't that what you hear?

Student: It seems that some of our wants are really harmless.

Dr. Hora: Are there harmless wants? It is interesting. Everybody would agree with you. It seems harmless, and yet it is not.

Student: How do we know that? (*Laughter*)

Dr. Hora: Good question. I was just thinking, *How could we clarify this fantastic thing?*

Student: Would you have to be aware of your wants and see how they play out in your experience? Because you want something, you get frustrated or angry.

Dr. Hora: Look here. Suppose you have a rubber doll. Have you ever had a rubber doll? This rubber doll you squeeze in one place—in the back, in the front. You squeeze this rubber doll. Under the pressure of your squeezing it, it becomes deformed until you release the pressure. Now, we are this rubber doll, and wanting is the pressure, which deforms us either physically, emotionally, or mentally. Even the slightest amount of wanting. Yes, suppose you want applesauce and you think about wanting applesauce. Something is happening in your stomach. Some kind of minimal, subliminal pressure. It strikes you: *It would be nice to have this applesauce on the chicken,* or something. Whenever we want something, this thought of wanting exerts a pressure in certain aspects of our life—physical, emotional, and any other kind. So you see, we cannot really afford to want anything. It is not helpful.

Now, if you ask people, they will say, "I want this. I want that. I want a promotion. I want to be famous. I want to be recognized. I want to be loved. I want to get, get, get this, get that"…right? We say it is natural. It is Christmastime. (*Laughter*) We want to *get.* So, the thought of wanting is the beginning of trouble. "The fear of the Lord is the beginning of wisdom" (Proverbs 9:10). Meta-psychiatry says it is the fear of not getting things we want. Then somebody has the experience of itchy feet—he wants something, and he cannot *not* want it. Suppose you have an itch someplace in your body, and you say, "The body says you want something." So, psychology says you have to *not* want what you want. That doubles the problem, because you are still wanting, and you are in conflict with your wanting. If we suffer from wanting, it will not help us to say, "I am not going to want this." Not wanting is also wanting. It is a dilemma.

Student: Is there a difference between wanting applesauce and needing nourishment?

Dr. Hora: Needing? You are looking for a legitimate want. (*Laughter*)

Student: It seems you need to eat.

Dr. Hora: Who said so? You are looking for a legitimate want. (*Laughter*)

Student: You couldn't say man needs to be loved or feel worthwhile? Is this kind of covering up a simple want?

Dr. Hora: Nobody needs to be loved. That is psychology. God says, "You are my image and likeness, and I am Love." How could you need anything? You are just glowing with love. "I am love, I am intelligence, I am power, I am perfection, I am freedom, I am joy, I am blessings." God says that about Himself, and whatever God says about Himself applies to us, because we are what God is. What if God were to say, "I am hungry (*laughter*)—I have a desire for cranberry sauce and turkey"? You see, now there are people who seek to legitimize their mental condition of wanting, and

there are people who seem to be ascetic who want to deny themselves, and they say, "I don't want"—but to want and to not want
is the same.

Student: There are so many beautiful things in the world, and there is
so much intelligence in the world. There is creativity, so many
expressions of Godlike qualities in various forms. So these are
blessings.

Dr. Hora: Blessings to those who can appreciate them.

Student: All right. So if all these things are there in visible form, aside
from the qualities that are not in visible form, what is wrong with
appreciating them? I don't know where the line is between wanting and appreciating. You don't want to just sit in your house and
know all these wonderful things are there and not be blessed by
the fact that they exist. What is the difference between wanting
and appreciating all these things? I don't know if I want to see
things or appreciate them or not. What is an existentially valid
way to be with regard to what we have been talking about?
(*Laughter*)

Dr. Hora: That is a good question—what is an existentially valid way
to be with regard to what we have been talking about? Who knows
the answer?

Student: I think you had said a couple of years ago that you do things
with pleasure, but not *for* pleasure. There is a difference based on
what your motivation truly is. I remember you telling us it is OK
to do things with pleasure. We are not against pleasure, as long as
it is not an end in itself.

Dr. Hora: Well, this is almost good. (*Laughter*) Any other contribu-
tions?

Student: Does it have anything to do with knowing the difference between an experience and a realization? If we want something, we

are involved in an experience, but if we are surrounded by beauty—it just seems like a qualitative difference. I am not sure of a practical example other than, when you are surrounded by beauty, you realize beauty. You see beauty, and you can appreciate that. But somehow when we want something and get something materially good, it doesn't have the same qualitative uplifting. It is just not satisfying, because you want something else right away. (*Laughter*) It is empty.

Student: Like if you go into a store and you see a beautiful vase and say, "It is beautiful," and you appreciate it, and you say, "I want it." (*Laughter*)

Student: When we were living in New York for the winter a couple of years ago, I remember asking this question in a private session. I said, "You know, it is such a lovely thing to go out for lunch and go to a museum or go out to a concert. There are so many things that you can do," and I said, "Is this self-confirmatory that one would like to be in a lovely place for lunch and one would like to do something?" And you said, "You *want* to do those things, and therefore..."

Dr. Hora: Do you know a good restaurant? (*Laughter*)

Student: If you are in New York City and you go to an opera, and you go with the intention of listening and appreciating a beautiful performance, I suppose it could be doing what God would want you to do, which is appreciating beauty. But if you go home and brag to your friends that you had the best seat, then the motive is off. Again, motive is the key to our behavior, whether it seems valid or not valid.

Dr. Hora: Buddha struggled with this problem. In his time, people struggled to find answers to the problems of life, and he accepted the teachings of Chuang-Tzu. Chuang-Tzu was a man who deprived himself of everything, every comfort he might desire, and went naked into the forest and lived there so that he could kill in himself all possible desires. His philosophy began evolving that the beginning of all suffering is desire. So he naturally deduced that if he could kill within himself all desires, he would become enlightened. He tried it for two years. After two years, he got fed up with this philosophy and said, "The hell with it. I am not going to do it. This is not the right approach." I bet you didn't know he said that! (*Laughter*)

Student: Suffering does come from desiring. Desire is wanting, and we do suffer. That part is OK, but the answer of going out to the woods and...

Dr. Hora: You mean, he overdid it. (*Laughter*)

Student: Metapsychiatry is not saying that is the answer.

Dr. Hora: We can say it to somebody whom we don't like. (*Laughter*)

Student: But you were saying that if we were able to overcome wanting, we would not suffer.

Dr. Hora: Yes, that is what the Buddha, too, said originally. You will be happy to hear there is one want that is legitimate, allowable, and good.

Student: Wanting not to want?

Dr. Hora: No, that is hell—when we want not to want, we are in hell. But there is a want that is legitimate: wanting to know the truth. "Ye shall know the truth." You cannot eat it. You have to know the truth, and the truth shall set you free (John 8:32). Buddha didn't know this. He just noticed that people who desired suffered; therefore, he proceeded with logical simplicity to say, "I am not going to desire. I will do everything possible to kill in myself desire." That was very naive of him—such a smart man. So, that is not going to help, but a sincere desire to know the truth will set us free. Jesus said so, and he knew about it, and you can believe him.

What does it mean to know the truth and to be liberated from wanting and not wanting—going to the concert or not going to the concert, going to the restaurant or not going to the restaurant, buying a vase or being vaseless? (*Laughter*) There is only one desire that is existentially valid. This is the sincere desire to know the truth; therefore, we speak of ourselves as being truth seekers. We seek the truth because the truth can set us free from wanting and from not wanting. Suppose we become truth seekers? What will happen then? We become students of Metapsychiatry (*laughter*)—legitimate, sincere students. Until that happens, we are just fooling around, trivializing the whole process. The truth must be fully appreciated as the will of God for man and the whole universe.

When they built the Hubble telescope, they wanted to go up to heaven to see what was there. Are they seeking the truth? Do you think they will be able to see the truth with the Hubble telescope? No? Anybody?

Student: They are just interested in the physical universe.

Dr. Hora: Will that help them to go to a better restaurant? All of these things really are frivolous and meaningless, because nobody will be healed and enlightened by looking into the Hubble telescope. They will come back and say there is nothing there. Like the Soviet astronauts: "We went all the way up in outer space, and I didn't see God anywhere." What do you think? There is a legitimate thing to want?

Student: I think it answers the original question in a way that you wouldn't have to ask the question. Are we going out to appreciate beauty, or are we going out as a distraction? The question doesn't even arise.

Dr. Hora: Of course not. Ye shall know the truth, and the truth shall make you free from wanting and not wanting. What is the big deal in that? All our problems—physical, mental, emotional, economic, political, racial—they come from wanting and not wanting, and there is no way of escaping this except the sincere, wholehearted interest in knowing the truth that can bring us peace and freedom and the wisdom of not hurting ourselves anymore with our wants and not-wants. We are all these rubber dolls, and every thought of wanting or not wanting creates a certain pressure in the rubber doll. We don't see it. We are not aware of it. We are constantly abusing ourselves with our thoughts about wanting and not wanting, and the only way we can be set free of this tendency of the human mind is by total commitment to being truth seekers. How does that work? Can a truth seeker go to a restaurant or eat cranberry sauce?

Student: Why not?

Dr. Hora: Good question. Can you answer it? So, what is the first principle of Metapsychiatry?

Student: "Thou shalt have no other interests before the good of God, which is spiritual blessedness."

Dr. Hora: What relevance does this have to what we were talking about?

Student: The words that come to my mind are that everything else is immaterial. The important thing is where the interest lies.

Dr. Hora: Yes, that is correct. How is that helpful?

Student: So if we are in the restaurant, we are acknowledging the good of God and spiritualizing the abundance, and we are grateful; it is beautiful, and it tastes good.

Dr. Hora: Sometimes it doesn't. (*Laughter*) "All things work together for good to them that love God" (Romans 8:28). So if we live by the First Principle, then wanting and not wanting will not be a source of torment for us. We will have the awareness of being blessed. What does it mean to be blessed? Is that pleasurable, being blessed?

Student: Is it a sense of wellness, that all is right in our world? A sense of PAGL?

Dr. Hora: All things tend to work together for good, and we are not tormented by thoughts of wanting or needing anything. There is no loneliness. There is no hunger for affection or love. None of these things disturb us anymore. There is peace, assurance, gratitude, and love.

Student: So when even very minor things don't seem to be working together for good, that is an immediate indication there is a want, and that throws a monkey wrench into what really is.

Dr. Hora: That's right. Sure. Isn't it wonderful to know this? I wonder what your cats will say. "Meow." (*Laughter*)

Student: I am still hung up between the notions of want and need, because I was under the impression that God knows what we need and those needs are always being met. So when the idea of a legitimate need begins to sneak in, even if we are trying to spiritualize it...I guess I want to ask if there is such a thing as a legitimate need.

Dr. Hora: There is only one legitimate need—to know the truth. And therefore we contemplate the truth continuously, day and night. That is ceaseless prayer, and it keeps us on the beam. Did you know that? Are you practicing that? We could also contemplate spiritual blessedness.

Now, what would happen if someone said, "I want spiritual blessedness"? We send him to Macy's and say, "Well, they have everything there. Go buy yourself some!"

Student: What is the difference between contemplating the truth and contemplating spiritual blessedness?

Dr. Hora: Almost nothing. Just a little bit. Because spiritual blessedness is already subjective. The truth is universal. See, it is possible for one individual to be conscious of blessedness and for another individual not to be, but the truth is a universal Reality of infinite mind, so that supersedes spiritual blessedness, which is just a by-product of seeking the truth. So the First Principle just says your interest must be in the good of God all the time—to know the truth. You cannot possess it, but you can appreciate it and know it more or less, and you can be aware that when you are sincerely focused on the Truth of Being, you will find that many things work out well in your life in a surprising way. You don't have to struggle for a parking spot or a great resolution in interpersonal conflicts. The world is so preoccupied with managing relationships. If you ever watch television, that is all they talk about. Everybody talks about relationships, and they want to do something about it. The more they try to harmonize relationships, the worse they get. It is self-defeating.

Student: When we are contemplating the Truth of Being, are we asking a question? Are we asking to know that?

Dr. Hora: Who would you ask about it—the police department? Who are you asking?

Student: You are asking to understand it, to realize it.

Dr. Hora: God doesn't tell us to beg. All these petitionary prayers are practiced in traditional religions, but this is ridiculous. It is like a fish asking another fish to give him some water. We don't have to beg God for anything. We have to know God. The Bible says, "This is life eternal that we may know thee, the only true God, and Jesus Christ, whom thou hast sent" (John 17:3). So we are truth seekers. We are not asking God to give us truth. That is ridiculous.

Student: Seeking is not the same as asking?

Dr. Hora: Of course not. It is interest focused in a certain direction. God is not a dispenser of truth. God *is* the truth. We cannot ask Him. We cannot tell Him anything.

Student: Then how do I know the truth?

Dr. Hora: How can we know whether we know the truth? Is there a way of knowing that this moment is a hallowed moment, that we know the truth? Is it possible for anybody to know that he knows, or is it just a gamble?

Student: PAGL consciousness.

Dr. Hora: Exactly. When we are conscious of PAGL, there is evidence that we are in touch with the truth, and that condition is called spiritual blessedness. Throughout the world people resort to petitionary prayers and perform all kinds of ceremonies to have an impact on God. It is very hard to get the guy to listen to us. (*Laughter*) Isn't that interesting? There is no way you can have a handle on God. It is no use trying.

Student: Can we just wait for PAGL?

Dr. Hora: You can wait if you want to, but you don't have to. (*Laughter*)

Student: But there is something we have to do. We have to turn our attention. We can't just think about it, which you mentioned recently. There is a difference between thinking about God and being aware of God. So when we sit down to contemplate the idea of God, we are seeking to understand the Truth of Being. You also said we seek to understand God as man. So we become aware of it instead of thinking about it.

Dr. Hora: That is it. Did you get it?

Student: I heard it. (*Laughter*)

Student: So it is invalid to say, "God help us."

Dr. Hora: Sure, of course. That is ridiculous. We do that. That is really revealing our naive idea about God. It is not a sin, but He doesn't hear it anyway. But it is good to turn attention to God as omnipotent, omnipresent Divine Mind, Love-Intelligence. If we contemplate life in the context of God in this manner, we will find that good things happen.

Student: Can you clarify what it means to seek to understand God as man?

Dr. Hora: "God as man." Who can explain it?

Student: When we see in man the qualities of God, and we are looking in man and seeing man as God's creation, the perfection of God, we are realizing God.

Dr. Hora: He got it right away. That's what an image and likeness of God is, God manifesting Himself through His individual creation, and there is "God as man." Yes? Now, it helps to think this way. What is the advantage of formulating it in this manner—"God as man"?

Student: We don't personalize our being.

Dr. Hora: You see, man is not God, but God manifests Himself through the enlightened consciousness of an individual man, and from time to time there have been individuals who have revealed this to the world.

Student: Could that be the meaning in the Bible of the term Jesus called himself, "the Son of Man"?

Dr. Hora: Jesus could appear to some people as the Son of Man and to more enlightened individuals as the Son of God.

Student: Is contemplation awareness?

Dr. Hora: Contemplation is the seeking of awareness. "God so loved the world, that he gave his only begotten Son, that whosoever believeth in him should not perish, but have everlasting life" (John 3:15-16).

7

Seeing God vs. Ignorance

Student: Dr. Hora, the other day I went to the supervisor's office to ask about some books I wanted to refer to. I couldn't find the books, so I was about to ask her, "Where are the books?" I couldn't find my voice, so I cleared my throat, but I still couldn't find my voice.

Dr. Hora: It was with the books, maybe.

Student: When I finally questioned her—"Where are the books?"—it came out in an unclear fashion. So I asked the meaning, and I think I bear some resentment toward this supervisor.

Dr. Hora: Right, right. So?

Student: I can't seem to get past resentment. So maybe this is the question: How does one transcend resentment toward this supervisor?

Dr. Hora: Before you say hello, you tell yourself not to be thinking of anything else. You remind yourself that right now you love her, and you are interested in remaining positively attuned to this individual.

Student: If I were to say something like that, I don't think I would understand it. And since I don't understand it, I fall into a nice-guy approach, which, from what I have seen, this woman takes

advantage of. "You do it; you're a nice guy." Yeah, I am a cooperative worker; I'll do it. Next, I find that this is what happens.

Dr. Hora: This is psychology. Did you know that you are an amateur
psychologist? It doesn't work; psychology doesn't work. But if
your reasoning is based on the acknowledgment of God as infinite
presence and Love-Intelligence, of which you are a representative,
this throws an entirely different light on the situation. We're not
interested in having nice relationships. We are interested in seeing
through the eyes of God, even before you say hello. Everything
works together for good to them that love being loving for God's
sake. It's nothing personal; you don't have to have a personal relationship with the supervisor. You have to be here for God. Life
is so much simpler that way, right? Relationships complicate life
terribly.

"I couldn't find my voice," you said. What a strange thing to say.
Where do you look for it? It was hidden; just like the books were
hidden, your voice was hidden—in a secret chamber of hostility
and judgmentalism. Right?

Student: Dr. Hora, he's talking about the fact that he harbors ill will
toward this woman. He doesn't like her; he's resentful. I understand what's required, but I don't understand how it happens. He
needs to see this woman differently, needs to say, "I love you."
But he doesn't mean it. So even if he says it anyway, but doesn't
mean it, it doesn't get him anywhere. As you say, it turns into
psychology. It doesn't work. He's angry because he says that now
she takes advantage of him. I'm the exact same way with other
people, but the solution that I end up with is just as bad as what
he's saying, because it's operational. So I do this and it doesn't
work. The notion of right seeing seems to be beyond my ability.
And anything that I try to substitute doesn't work, because it's all
operational. When I go to see this person I'm going to say I love
him. So I say to myself, "I love him." But I *don't* love him. I keep

saying I love him but—how can you love somebody that you don't love? That's the issue.

Dr. Hora: Well, you need a new pair of glasses. We have to learn to look at life and at people and situations through the eyes of God, not through the eyes of personal opinions. You could also say, "Before I say hello, I have to remind myself of how God sees the individual. I have to see this individual through the eyes of God." Immediately things change. We change. They change. They become what they really are, and we become what we really are, and we become divinely governed. Suddenly, all anxiety disappears. All tension disappears. Suddenly we find our voice; it's right there. We found it. We find the books. Now there is good will on both sides, on every side. Then that's a wonderful situation. There is no need for tension and anxiety in personal relationships. This word "relationship" is anathema to God. There are no "relationships." Relationships are on a seesaw. You know the seesaw? One goes up; the other goes down. All it is is mental strife, a battle for power and superiority of all kinds. So you have to learn to see life through the eyes of God. How does God see life? Perfect. He created it. God created a perfect universe and peopled it with reflections of Himself. And that's what we have to learn.

Student: So it seems like in this context we get stymied in attempting this by being inauthentic. I may dislike or resent this individual, but if I hear what's being said correctly, it's that there is a much healthier way of looking at things. The other way of looking at things, the relationship way, is always troublesome.

Dr. Hora: Right.

Student: And if we genuinely explore this way of looking at things, then we will see that things will work out.

Dr. Hora: Right, sure. Did everybody hear what he said? It's very true.

Student: I'd like to follow up on what he just said. Sometimes if I become aware of a thought that was expressed by the other students, I can recognize the invalidity of it. And I get a little frightened by the invalid thought, because it's so clear that invalid thoughts have meanings and that meanings express themselves in our lives in very negative ways. So, that's one thing that sort of pushes me in a different direction. But it doesn't seem quite right; it's almost like you're searching for God out of fear. So that doesn't seem quite right. And then I think that you need to just turn to God, because that's the way it is. And you can't fight what is.

Dr. Hora: The Bible says: "The fear of the Lord is the beginning of wisdom" (Proverbs 9:10). This was always very puzzling to people. It still is, as if we would have to be afraid of God.

Student: Well, no, I'm not afraid of God. I'm afraid of invalid thoughts.

Dr. Hora: Godlessness. What we have to be afraid of is Godlessness.

Student: But you said that what the student said is very true, that these thoughts are troublesome. Isn't that wrong too, to seek a better way because of being fearful of invalid thoughts?

Dr. Hora: Well, it's not wrong, but it's inevitable. That's what Metapsychiatry teaches, that we have to be aware of the thoughts that are present in consciousness, their quality and direction and source, everything about them. We need to seek to bring our attention into focus with Divine Reality. That's all there is. But when you said "the fear," you were referring to the Bible speaking of the fear of the Lord. No, that is a mistake. We don't have to be afraid of God; we have to be afraid of Godlessness. And when we are involved in personality conflicts, there is no God in our consciousness at that point. And then mistakes happen. There is fear, anxiety, and tension; there is confusion. So we have to be afraid of Godlessness, interaction thinking, self-confirmatory thinking. This is a distraction from God, which is called the Devil. The function of the Devil is to distract us from the awareness of God and His universe of perfect being. So, when the student has an encounter with a supervisor, they are completely involved in thoughts of relationship, which can be negative or positive. God is not in the picture. Nobody is aware of God. And losing awareness of God is a mistake, a grave mistake. So we have to maintain constant conscious awareness of God through perfect love and sincere contemplation of the truth of being. With a little luck, this is possible. A little bit of luck. Get me to the church on time. (*Laughter*)

People will ask, "What has Metapsychiatry to offer that all of these tremendous volumes of books about psychology, psychoanalysis, psychotherapy, psycho-this and psycho-that, cannot offer? What have they got that other people haven't got? In what way is this teaching different from all the dignified and admired and erudite and highly respected volumes of books and teachings throughout the world? Why bother with Metapsychiatry?" You can be on Fifth Avenue, on Park Avenue, in elegant surroundings in some prestigious salons, with people respected throughout the world for their writings, and thousands of people go to see these people. I heard recently about a professor of economics, a lady professor of economics at New York University, with a husband who was also a prestigious academic. They were going to a very elegant place for psychoanalysis for years and years, and they were always getting worse and worse. They cannot live without each other; without each other they were economically sliding down into a pit. And nothing seems to work. It's no surprise, because without God nothing can work, since God runs the universe. And if you ignore God's presence in His own universe, where are you? You're in never-never land. In Metapsychiatry, we learn to see through the eyes of God and to maintain a constant conscious awareness of God's presence as a governing intelligence of life. And we are alert not to allow anything else to distract us from the awareness of God, which is the work of the . That's what the Devil is here for, to distract us. But then, if there were no Devil, we wouldn't appreciate the glorious spiritual blessedness of the children of God. Before you say hello, you remind yourself that you're not just another person meeting another person, and managing a relationship. You don't manage a relationship. "Is you is or is you ain't?" That's the question, right?

Student: Now, I could complain that I have difficulty seeing God in this situation. But I could also say it another way, that I am more interested in fostering and hanging on to my resentment than in seeing things in a more spiritual way. Would that be more correct?

Dr. Hora: Well, it's a free country. You can hang on to any kind of matter you like, but does God hang on to resentment? God forbid. Remember that you are not what you seem to be. You are not a human person indulging himself in resentful feelings and thoughts. You are a transparency for God. It is the Father that dwelleth in you, He doeth the works. And as far as your resentments are concerned, you ain't never was nothin'. So we don't have to manage our feelings and emotions and opinions and relationships. We don't have to be involved in this human misery. We just need to learn to see who we really are, the truth of being. And that's what is. And everything that really is was made by God and is God and is perfect. "Be ye therefore perfect, even as your Father...in heaven is perfect" (Matthew 5:48). We don't have to make ourselves perfect; we already are perfect. God made us perfect. And in Metapsychiatry, we learn to see this.

Student: Dr. Hora, you are using the word "Devil." Is there a definition of the Devil, or is that a symbol of whatever is not godly? What is the Devil?

Dr. Hora: It's a personification of the evil desire to ignore God. He has two horns and a three-pronged pitchfork. And Christmas is coming soon, and you will see him all over the place.

Student: It starts at Thanksgiving.

Dr. Hora: Yes.

Student: Dr. Hora, when you said before that we have to see ourselves as perfect, how does one see oneself as perfect nonpersonally? How would you regard yourself?

Dr. Hora: Well, you are contemplating the Truth of Being. The Truth of Being is not a physical person; it's a Divine consciousness. And that consciousness is supremely intelligent and loving and absolutely perfect—never born, never dying, hid with Christ in God. It already is. Don't worry. This is good. It is absolutely perfect. As the Bible puts it, nothing can be put into it nor taken away from it.

Student: What is it that sees it?

Dr. Hora: God is seeing Himself. He has a mirror. He is always looking in a mirror, and he sees Himself. If you have children, you very often see yourself in your children, don't you?

Student: I think a mother probably would.

Dr. Hora: The good and the bad and the stupid and the smart and the male and the female. But we are transparencies through whom God is manifesting Himself in the world through an infinite variety of individualities. If the ocean is the spirit, then a snowflake is the soul of an individual. What's the difference between the ocean and the snowflake? It's the same substance. The snowflake has the same substance as the ocean. And yet every snowflake is an individual, and different from every other snowflake. Isn't that interesting? Are we all flaky? (*Laughter*) Some people will say...

Student: Nondimensional spiritual consciousness exists regardless of a dimensional being?

Dr. Hora: Yes. What happens to a snowflake if it melts and falls into the ocean?

Student: It becomes part of the ocean.

Dr. Hora: Did you ever think of it—what happens to that individual uniqueness that every snowflake is?

Student: It disappears, right?

Dr. Hora: It seems to, but it couldn't possibly. Either it is a unique individual or it isn't. And if a soul is immortal, and even if its formal appearance disappears, still it cannot be lost; it must exist. So if somebody dies and he disappears, we say the soul is immortal and it survives, but we cannot see it because it's nondimensional. I think in computer memories interesting things can happen. Information can disappear, right? And there's no way of seeing it and knowing it except if you know how to call it back, right? And that interferes in its perfection. And while it was in the computer, it was nothing, right? There was no way anybody could see it.

Student: Have you experienced this?

Dr. Hora: No, I've listened to my friend who talks computerese. That's a new language. It's fascinating.

Student: It's really interesting because it's invisible.

Dr. Hora: Yes, nobody would suspect that it is there, right? Sometimes you get surprised by what's coming to you.

Student: Dr. Hora, when you said "What is it when a snowflake goes into the ocean?" the first thing that came to mind is bliss.

Dr. Hora: Bliss?

Student: Bliss. But if the analogy is that we're really part of God but we're really separate, if we were to see that, it would be blissful.

Dr. Hora: Blissful, certainly. Of course the quality of Divine life is spiritual bliss. Bliss consciousness. Or, as the First Principle says, "Thou shalt have no other interests before the good of God, which is spiritual blessedness." When we are in a state of spiritual blessedness, everything seems to be all right. There is nothing to complain about or worry about or be afraid of. Peace, assurance, gratitude, love. This is the supreme good of life. Lasagna notwithstanding.

Student: I'd like to consider the word "PAGL" in a situation like a meeting where people are feeling very pressured. In a meeting where, for instance, a report has to get generated and calculated, and it has to be done by a certain time, because people urgently need this report. There is a lot of politics going on at the meeting, and everyone is jockeying to show they know more than other people. It's a very ugly situation. How can one be aware of God in that situation? It's not that difficult when you're by yourself, but in a meeting with these people where all these things are going on, how can one be aware of God?

Dr. Hora: That's a very good question. Any answers? He describes life as it is experienced in the marketplace, right? In the marketplace, that's how we experience life. But experiences are not real life. Experiences are what we perceive; we perceive the thoughts in the sea of mental garbage. So, how can one transcend these experiences and still remain in business?

Student: Not become a priest.

Student: Deal with the issues, rather than with personalities?

Dr. Hora: Oh, absolutely, that's an absolute requirement. The question is, could an enlightened individual function in a meeting place, in a bank or anywhere else, where normal human crazy people communicate? That's the big, big question. And sometimes it's difficult. Perhaps most of the time it is very difficult. But you can always excuse yourself and go to a private place and contemplate the Truth of Being and come back refreshed with new ideas. (*Laughter*)

Student: Well, last week in our private session, I asked you, "How could contemplating the Truth of Being help us transcend what you're describing?" And you said that the Truth of Being is perfect God and perfect man, and that if you're contemplating perfect God and you stick with it, then you begin to see that you can't be anything other than that perfection that God is. You just stay with this until you can in some way see that you are in fact that perfection that God is. And you said that would be a helpful way to function, I guess.

Dr. Hora: Yes. Pretty soon the fear leaves you. See, in such situations people are constantly thrashing at each other, competing with each other, and intimidating each other. Now, if you can turn your thoughts to the perfection of God and His universe, this gives you new strength. The fear leaves you, and you are not upset over what people want. All these things can leave you, and suddenly you are normal again.

Student: Well I'm hopeful that something you said tonight makes it easier for me, because I found it impossible to look at somebody at the meeting and see that person as perfect. It seems to me that you have to be God to see that person as perfect. But tonight you said that another approach might be, instead of saying, "I love you" and not being able to mean it, another way of approaching it would be to think of this person the way God sees this person.

That, I think, would be easier for me. In other words, I can understand, I think, a little bit how God could see this person as perfect even if I can't. So the fact that I can't, I find it so frustrating all the time. I find terrible frustration that I cannot see these other people as perfect or myself as perfect. But I think it may be easier then to see these people the way I can understand that God sees them.

Dr. Hora: Right. This reminds me of a guy who was negotiating with a very high-powered manufacturer of elevators. And this fellow tried to negotiate a contract with the elevator guy, who was very rough and arbitrary, and they couldn't agree on some detail. They left all frustrated that the deal was an impossibility. This fellow complained that it seemed impossible because this man was so arbitrary and didn't budge. He never wanted to consider any alternative. It was very upsetting for him, right? And then we talked for a while and threw a new light on the situation and brought God into the picture. And next week, this arbitrary, dictatorial fellow initiated a new negotiation phase, and he was friendly and cooperative, and the thing was resolved, because God, the third party, was in the negotiation. If God isn't there, nothing can work. But if you invite God into the negotiating room, you will see the difference. Right? He was that guy.

Student: You never forget him, either.

Dr. Hora: If you go into negotiation with someone about business or something, and if you assume that this process must be adversarial, then you have already built in the factor of failure, because adversarial negotiations never can come to a favorable resolution. But before you say hello, you remind yourself, "This is not an adversarial situation. We're not adversaries. We are spiritual beings seeking the truth that makes everything harmonious and blesses one and blesses the other equally." This whole concept of adversarial negotiations and debating is based on the assumption that *"homo homini lupus"* What is that? What is that? Nobody knows Latin here?

Student: Something about the wolves?

Dr. Hora: Wolf, Yes. Arnold Wolf—no. Men are with each other like wolves, like animals. Adversarial, hostile, power-mad, destructive. That's the whole concept of an adversary. Adversarial relationship—lawyers have invented it.

Student: Dr. Hora, I'd like to ask a little more about the issue of our uniqueness and when the student said that her first response to the image of the snowflake melting into the ocean was bliss. It seems that I tend to get uniqueness and personhood very confused in my mind. For example, is the Buddha nature when there is a total loss of a sense of self? Does holding on to the idea of bliss, as I heard the other student say, come because it really is a relinquishing of selfhood? But uniqueness and selfhood are just inextricably mixed up in my understanding.

Dr. Hora: Yes. Nobody mentioned selfhood in a psychological sense. We're not selves in a psychological way, because self is synonymous with personhood, and we're not persons, either. But there is a sense, a sense of selfhood, in terms of the uniqueness of each individual. So like a snowflake, every one of us is a creation of God, and everyone is different and yet made of the same stuff. It's like in the Bible there is reference to "[T]he leaves of the tree were for the healing of the nations" (Revelation 22:2). That's a mysterious kind of statement. Are they recommending that we use the leaves and put them on roofs? People actually used to do that. But this is a naive idea. How can you heal the nations of the world with leaves from a tree, right? It must have a secret meaning. All of the apocalypses were loaded with symbolism that is difficult to understand—it takes a great deal of meditation and study to come to some realization. What is meant by this, "[T]he leaves of the tree are for the healing of the nations?" The Metapsychiatric view of this mysterious thing is that we have to contemplate what a leaf is. The knowledge of what the leaf is, the Truth of the Being of the leaf, can illuminate for us the healing of nations. Namely, you have to understand that every leaf—and there might be a million leaves, let's say, on a sugar maple tree—every leaf is different from every other leaf. They are all unique, and they never fight except when the wind blows. They coexist harmoniously on that tree, and they are made of the same stuff as the tree is made of, and they identify the tree. They have their own identity, and they are unique, and at the same time they are all maple leaves. So we can understand this complicated fact of nature, this phenomenon. A tree teaches us to see that there is such a thing as unique individuality. We're not speaking of self but of unique individuality of soul. And the soul is made of the spirit, *is* the spirit, just like the snowflake is a uniquely individual manifestation that is made of the same substance as the ocean. Now if it disappears into the ocean, the question is, "Where is it?" Like with the computer— once you commit something to the computer's memory, it disappears. There is no way you can see it anymore. But you can record it. And probably that's what happens to snowflakes, too. Next winter, you have to shovel them. So, if the nations of the world would understand the leaf, the whole world would be healed. The leaves are for the healing of nations. What is needed for the nations is to understand the leaf, and that understanding of the leaf will enlighten the whole world, and consequently there will be universal PAGL. Right? PAGL consciousness in the world— wouldn't that be nice? To understand the leaf. There was an Indian guru who said that enlightenment happens to you when you can see the Taj Mahal in a blade of grass. Isn't that an interesting saying? "You can see the Taj Mahal in a blade of grass."

Student: What does the Taj Mahal represent?

Dr. Hora: Good question. That's what you have to answer. Then you will understand this koan. What does the Taj Mahal represent?

Perfection, architectural perfection; love, because love has built it; beauty, perfect beauty—that's the Taj Mahal. Only the Divine Mind could have given rise to such an architectural miracle. And a blade of grass is an architectural miracle that grows spontaneously by the grace of God. Now, if you truly understand such things, you're enlightened. The leaves of the tree are for the healing of the nations. When we speak of healing in Metapsychiatry, we are always speaking of the quality of consciousness. When we heal, there is only one disease; it's called ignorance. And when ignorance is healed, it is eliminated from consciousness—then you have a healing. What happens when a leaf is severed from the tree?

Student: It dies.

Dr. Hora: It dies. What does that mean? It ceases to be a leaf; it becomes trash. Without God, everything is trash.

Student: Even when our body dies?

Dr. Hora: Our body is trash, surely. Ashes to ashes, dust to dust. But the soul is immortal and lives on in the ocean of Love-Intelligence. There's the sea of mental garbage, right? And the ocean of Love-Intelligence.

8

Spiritual Backsliding/Addiction

Student: Dr. Hora, we come to this class and we study or seek to learn the truth, and although there is a lot of truth still to be discovered, it does seem in my experience that I have learned some of the truth. And yet, I leave here and I find that I don't put it into practice daily, and I always find myself resorting to reminding myself of the three "Rs." The question that comes to mind is: Can somebody start just relying on the three "Rs"—allowing oneself just to slide back, indulging in interaction thinking and self-confirmatory thinking, and then…it sort of seems there has to be a limit in some way or other to how many times this can happen and it can still be a sincere quest.

I guess another way of putting it would be, if I were in ignorance of the truth…of course, compassion and understanding seem like the right way to look at any individual. But when there seems to be a growth in understanding and yet regularly you see it not being applied, or not always leading your thoughts and behavior…it seems almost easier to have compassion for the ignorant individual than it is to have compassion for someone who has had the opportunity to study the truth.

Dr. Hora: Yes. So what is the question?

Student: I was trying to think how to formulate it in having to do with—I don't know what you call it—backsliding, or just simply turning away from the truth, and bringing your thoughts back into focus. Over a long period of time it begins to feel like it's a vicious cycle as opposed to growth that is happening, where you are aware of the truth of the situation and then five minutes later find yourself completely involved in the interaction of the situation.

Dr. Hora: Yes. So what is the question?

Student: The only thing I can think of is—can you wear out the three "Rs"? (*Laughter*)

Dr. Hora: Eventually. (*Laughing*)

Student: And then what?

Dr. Hora: Eventually we all wear out. (*Laughing*)

Student: Dr. Hora, would that question be whether after studying a number of years, one can feel discouraged? Maybe one can get more self-confirmatory guilt, thinking, *I should know better by now.*

Dr. Hora: "I should?"

Student: After many years, I guess I understand that sometimes you get involved in a mistake where something happens, and to compound that you start thinking that happened to me, I mean—*By now, after all these years…*

Dr. Hora: That is how the insurance companies speculate. They say to you, "In twelve sessions you have to cure this person" (*laughing*). But we are not here for a cure. Is anybody sick? There is no sickness, and there is no cure. What are we here for?

Student: To come to know the truth.

Dr. Hora: I knew a man who came here for an ingrown toenail. (*Laughter*) So I sent him downstairs to the podiatrist (*laughing*). That solved his problem. He didn't have to come here.

Student: Maybe there's another way to describe what seems like a problematic situation. I will sometimes find myself indulging in just interaction thinking, and my internal observer sees that I have been indulging in interaction thinking and knows better, but on it goes. And again, if there were ignorance of the fact that there was another alternative, then I could just happily go ahead and enjoy it. (*Laughter*) But the issue of the awareness—whether it is a reluctance, or whether it is laziness, or whether it is another form of temptation—the idea of being susceptible again just comes back to the issue: "Well, when I do turn to the truth, and even when in this particular instance benefits accrue, then how or why is it that the interaction thinking seems to be there the next time?"

Dr. Hora: How or why. This is double jeopardy (*laughing*).

Student: Something happened to me today that seems to recur as my problem. I made a mistake and I blamed someone else for the mistake, and I realized that it was my mistake. But I got angry at the other person and I yelled or whatever, and it was not until later on that I apologized, and I realized as it was going on that I shouldn't be (*laughter*)—that I *need not* be—yelling at this person (*laughter*). I think it has to do with the fear of being embarrassed or blamed for doing something wrong.

Dr. Hora: That is why you do it (*laughing*).

Student: That is why I do it. And I continue to do it.

Dr. Hora: Nobody has forbidden you to engage in interaction thinking. This is a free country (*laughing*). Either we understand or we think of it as some kind of a prohibition. In Metapsychiatry, we are not forbidden anything. We can even dance with girls. (*Laughter*)

Student: As long as we are not interested. (*Laughter*)

Dr. Hora: So she is really asking the question, "What is the meaning of backsliding?" It's a nice snowfall today. We can slide backward and forward (*laughing*). Yes, everybody experiences backsliding from time to time. The difference between you and others is that you are aware of it, and you can stop it. You can turn your interest to more wholesome ways of coexisting with your fellow man. So that is the difference. Other people just go on merrily around, interacting left and right and having fun, and we don't have this fun, especially if we have a tendency toward controlling ourselves. We are not here to control anything or anybody, not even ourselves. We are perfectly free to be out of control.

There is a strange situation here that we are in. We may be studying for years and years, and we know all that is written in the books, and we know what is valid and what is not valid—and yet we experience backsliding, which can be of various degrees, and always there is a price to be paid for backsliding. People who don't study Metapsychiatry don't realize that they are hurting themselves with backsliding, but we know that, and we still do backsliding, which means that we don't know well enough.

Now, the insurance company will say, "Well, how long will it take for you to learn not to backslide?" (*Laughter*) There is something wrong with the theory—absolutely it is wrong, because it doesn't apply to human beings (*laughing*). We cannot settle down and say, "It is just human." You are not supposed to be human. You are not supposed to be normal. You are not learning here to be normal. We are learning to be spiritual. What does it mean? That we only drink whiskey with soda—spirits? (*Laughing*) So the rules of the world, which are a great source of tribulation to most people— they do not apply to students of Metapsychiatry. Jesus said we are in this world, but we are not of it. We are not human persons. He said, "Be of good cheer; [it is possible to] overcome the world,"[6] and the first step in overcoming the world is what?

Student: You have to know what the world is to overcome it.

Dr. Hora: How do we find out what the world is?

Student: Through suffering. (*Laughter*)

Dr. Hora: The world is made of two elements—very simple, right? Yes and no (*laughing*). It is made of interaction thinking and self-confirmatory ideation. These are the basic elements that constitute the world. And if we are to overcome the world, we have to learn to live above these levels of worldly seeing and acting. So, if we are backsliding, it is just normal and human, but we wouldn't want to practice it. It is like driving without paying attention to the traffic regulations or the red light. Even if you could drive happily, you wouldn't get very far. So you would get hurt, and so it is— why bother to overcome the world? Why, indeed? Most people never even think of it; they just merrily go around fighting with everybody over anything and experiencing all kinds of injuries from the world. So that is the way it is with backsliding. We cannot blame anybody. Nobody can help us. We can be alert and understand that there is a better way to survive in this world, by overcoming the world and by understanding that you cannot just settle down and say it is only normal. Most people would say it is only normal, right? We cannot say that. "Normal" is no solution. It is normal to be ignorant. It is normal to get hurt. If you would settle down to "normal," then you wouldn't have to come here and study all these complicated things, which are essentially not complicated but very intelligent and reasonable and understandable, and it is possible to live harmoniously this way.

---

[6] "In the world ye shall have tribulation: but be of good cheer; I have overcome the world" (John 16:33).

Very often it is the husband or the wife who is discontented. "Look here," says the husband to his wife, "You have been seeing Hora for 25 years, and you still don't know how to make scrambled eggs!" (*Laughing*) There is a student of Metapsychiatry who is being pressured by her husband to take Prozac. Do you know what Prozac is? It is a drug. She was in Mount Sinai Hospital psychiatric care, and they are feeding her this drug Prozac. This is a drug that is legal and that therefore is very popular. You don't have to be afraid of getting arrested. You feel good by taking Prozac, and it is cheap. It is $2 a pill. I asked this patient, "Why does your husband pressure you to take a drug?" And she is a very intelligent young lady, and she said, "He wants me to take this drug because then he will feel better." He wants his wife to become a drug addict so that he can feel good.

There was a time when psychiatry was a very cruel process. There were married couples who forced one another to have lobotomies so that they could feel better. The idea was that if you perform a lobotomy on your husband, then he won't be nagging you, and you will feel better—but he gets crippled for life. And now it is with drugs. It is either the insurance company—it is going to be so that the insurance companies will really control the health care system. They have the money. They will be in a position to dictate to the doctor how to prescribe and how to treat his patients. All kinds of things will develop. "I am the husband; I have a right to say what kind of treatment my wife should have." It sounds reasonable. "I have to live with her." Right? But it can develop into wholesale tyranny. People will tyrannize each other, and the insurance companies will really control the whole process.

Student: That brings up a question about knowing—sometimes we think we know what is good for somebody.

Dr. Hora: Oh yes, sure—not sometimes, but very often. (*Laughter*)

Student: And also maybe…well, it is hard enough to know what is good for us.

Dr. Hora: Yes; therefore we have a great choice of thousands of treatment methods available to us. You can go to this one and that one. You can go through famous clinics, like the Mayo Clinic, and such-and-such hospital. It is a bewildering choice. It is more like choosing an automobile. Some people have a hard time choosing a car…and people have a hard time understanding what is required to be well, to reach a point where one can be well. And what does it mean to be well? You see, if you take a pill, you will feel well for a few hours. There are many, many ways people try to find valid ways of being well. And what does it mean to be well?

Student: Well, maybe one of the biggest mistakes we make is we think in terms of physical wellness, like "There won't be any pain," or we think in terms of social wellness: "We won't get into conflict."

Dr. Hora: Right; the husband wants to have a happy wife—so let her take Prozac. He has a right to say, "Well, I am entitled to a happy wife."

Student: Also with children. I have had children in class who were on constant medication. Not Prozac, but there is something they use to calm down children. The children take it constantly.

Dr. Hora: Right. Everything that you take into the body has a side effect. There has never yet been any drug or pill or medicine without any side effects. There was a time when people were hooked on Valium. Have you ever heard of Valium? This was a tranquilizer that seemingly had no side effects and relieved anxiety and made people feel good, except it had cumulative effects. People got hooked on the Valium, and after a year or two the side effects began to show, and nowadays you don't hear about Valium. People don't take it much anymore because it was discovered that it was not innocuous. So now there are—I understand six million are already hooked on Prozac. Imagine six million pills every day. It is $12 million. The pharmaceutical company that invented this is getting constant cash flow of $12 million daily. (*Laughter*) It is a wonderful business. No wonder it is spreading like wildfire. Everybody wants to take this, but it is not a solution.

Now, if it is slippery outside, you walk cautiously, right? It is advisable to walk cautiously. If we are backsliding, it is advisable to live cautiously, which means mindfulness of the fact that interaction thinking and acting is invalid and is harmful. So what is required is to be mindful. Nobody can do it for you. You have to look out, because when you walk on the street today, nobody can stop you from backsliding. You have to walk carefully and drive carefully.

Student: I was just putting together some things in the last week or so. The holiday season tends to be a very rushed season, and certainly the opportunities for interaction are very great. Speaking of going cautiously, I just realized in the last week I think I bumped my head maybe five times. I think this is a wake-up call of some sort.

Dr. Hora: Absolutely.

Student: You once mentioned that initially we are driven to the truth by our suffering, and at some point perhaps we reach a stage where we are drawn to the truth. But it is hard to understand what makes that difference.

Dr. Hora: Without guidance, we will never be drawn to the truth. We will be drawn from one pill to another, from one doctor to another, from one system to another, endlessly. There is an infinite supply of invalid solutions. We can never exhaust it all. How many valid answers are there to the question of how much is two and two? You could have a million invalid answers and only one valid answer. So it is with being well. To be well means to be able to see what is valid and what is not valid. If we can see what is valid, this is called enlightenment. What does that word mean? It means "seeing the light." It is very simple. We need to see the light and to focus our attention on it all the time.

Student: So that is mindfulness. That is what you mean by mindfulness: awareness, rather than just knowing about something and treating it, as you said, as a prohibition or that "we shouldn't."

Dr. Hora: You can agree with it. You can disagree with it. That is not it, when you just know about it. You have to really see it, and then it is very simple.

Once I worked with a Jesuit priest from whom I learned a lot about Catholicism. He told me that they have a system that helps them not to backslide into sinful ways of living. The system is, you go to your bishop and request to be beaten by a whip called a cat-o'-nine-tails—a whipping was supposed to be protection against backsliding. Just another one of these remedies. (*Laughter*) So I said to him, "Don't you get addicted to these beatings?" He said yes (*laughing*). You can get hooked on it, and then it is called religious masochism (*laughing*). There is no protection against backsliding except a deeper, clearer understanding of what the issue is.

Student: I don't know if it is a cure, but at any rate, an answer to backsliding might be new suffering. If you are backsliding and then suddenly you find yourself suffering, then you are more willing to turn your interest, because now you have this situation that is causing you pain.

Dr. Hora: Yes.

Student: Would you say it requires, almost always, a new form of suffering?

Dr. Hora: Well, pain is inevitable but not necessary. The pain will not cure the problem. It will wake us up to the realization that something is wrong, and we may look for a better solution. A cat-o'-nine-tails is not a cure for backsliding. In the Middle Ages, they did all kinds of gruesome things to people in the name of the truth and for the love of Christ. There were beatings. There were tortures. There was imprisonment and ostracism. There were all kinds of things. Today we use chemical means to improve the human race (*laughing*). But there is always backsliding.

Human beings are essentially addictive life forms. Everybody has a tendency toward becoming addicted, whether it is to food or drugs or sex. It is amazing how much sexual abuse we hear about nowadays. It is as if a hidden contagious sex disease invaded and pervaded civilization. When I first learned about AIDS as a sexually transmitted disease, I thought, *Now it is the end of the sexual revolution.* I even said it: "This is the end of the sexual revolution." No…it had no effect. It didn't slow it down. It is rampant. Sex mania is rampant. Nobody will give up sex to save his life. So the human condition is extremely ignorant and even self-destructive, because you can get addicted even to beatings or punishments.

Parents know very well that they cannot punish children when they misbehave. If you punish them, they get worse. And the educational systems and the legal systems, the justice system—nothing works. Absolutely nothing works. Only the truth works, but the truth must be truthful. He who would seek the truth has to become truthful about the truth, because there are many people who lie with the truth, and Jesus knew that. He said, "Thou art a liar, and the father of it."[7] We are lying; therefore, the truth has not much effect on us because we are lying to ourselves and we

---

[7] "Ye are of *your* father the devil, and the lusts of your father ye will do. He was a murderer from the beginning, and abode not in the truth, because there is no truth in him. When he speaketh a lie, he speaketh of his own: for he is a liar, and the father of it" (John 8:44).

are always looking for solutions that would somehow bridge the gap between truth and the lie.

Student: Dr. Hora, would you please give us an example of how we lie to ourselves?

Dr. Hora: Well, suppose you find that if you have a glass of wine with your meal, you feel better. You know that there will be a price for alcohol, and you are lying that it will not hurt. This is normal. Everybody does it, right? Yes. We tell ourselves lies.

Student: We know better, and yet we do something that is not healthy.

Dr. Hora: We are lying to ourselves, yes.

Student: How can you do something—way back you said "and not be interested"? Can you drink a glass of wine without interest? (*Dr. Hora laughs*)

Dr. Hora: You see, it is interesting that he always reveals the way his thoughts work. He wants to be able to drink wine (*laughter*) without any alcohol content.

Student: No, I would like clarification on how you can engage in something and not be interested in it.

Dr. Hora: By lying to yourself.

Student: So that is an invalid statement.

Dr. Hora: Of course (*laughing*). What is that saying? "You can fool some people some of the time, but you cannot fool all of the people all of the time"—and certainly you cannot fool the divine principle of sobriety. The Bible says, "Be sober and vigilant, for the Devil, as a roaring lion, walketh about, seeking whom he may devour."[8] I have never heard the Devil, but the Devil works in

---

[8] "Be sober, be vigilant; because your adversary the devil, as a roaring lion, walketh about, seeking whom he may devour" (Peter 5:8).

subtle ways. He is also called "the whisperer." You hear a certain voice in the back of your mind: "Do it. It won't hurt you. It is fine. Everybody else is doing it. It is OK. Take this pill and take that pill. It will be all right."

Student: If you are addicted to certain invalid thoughts, are you lying to yourself, or are you unable to overcome it?

Dr. Hora: You say, "It won't hurt me." Every drug addict starts out with marijuana and will say, "Well, this is innocuous, and besides, other people may get addicted, but *I* won't get addicted. I can take it. I can resist it. It cannot hurt me." Most of the time, you hear these rationalizations. We are convinced that we cannot get hooked on anything. The fact is we can get hooked on everything, even a vegetable—baseball, cigarettes, and all kinds of things. We are always in danger of getting attached to something—person, place, or thing—and the moment we are attached to something, we are in a state of idolatry. What does "idolatry" mean?

Student: It means we have made something that is not God into our god.

Dr. Hora: Into our god—personal god—and it takes control of our lives. Once a cat came to our house and was knocking on the window. He insisted on being let in. But we didn't want to have a cat in the house. Every day he would come, and one day we gave him a bowl of food because he was starving, and I was standing far away. He ate ravenously, and when he noticed that I was watching him, he dropped the food and came running to me and rubbed himself on my feet as if saying, "I love you more than the food." I got hooked. (*Laughter*) We took him in, and pretty soon this cat was running our life. (*Laughter*) He would start meowing at 3:00 in the morning—he wanted to go out. At 3:15, he was meowing that he wanted to come in, and after a while we were completely under his control, always amazed about his intelligence. This beautiful cat—but you see, we yielded, and he took over. We had to give him away. The people who took him from us were cat lovers, and the first thing this cat did was, he jumped on the head of the household and developed a habit of sitting on his shoulder, and this flattered the man so much, he immediately fell in love with this cat—and the cat of course took over that household, and so it is with addiction. We get hooked on something, and we love it. We like it, and we cannot be without it.

Student: I think we are always blaming ourselves. I think that might be part of the original question. You can see it in others. You see the cat on the man's shoulder and say, "I recognize this"—but sometimes when we look at ourselves we say, "I should know better." How do we have greater compassion—establish compassion for ourselves? When we talk about compassion, it always seems like it is for others. We need compassion for ourselves, not to blame ourselves for backsliding.

Dr. Hora: OK. So how can we be protected from addiction—getting bonded? The psychologists call it "bonding." Isn't that nice? You get bonded to the cat, to the dog. You get bonded. It means that you've found a certain self-confirmatory experience in that situation, and you enjoy thinking of yourself, *Well, the cat loves me; I must be a good guy. This dog is crazy about me; he follows me around.* And you begin to feel proud of what a wonderful person you are because the cat loves you. But if you understand the process of so-called bonding, or addiction, then you can take a different view of the situation. We can love animals, but we don't have to be attached to them, and we can love our fellow human beings, our spouses, and we don't have to be attached to them. We see them as God's creatures, and then there will be no complications.

Student: What usually happens is that we become attached or addicted to something before we have an opportunity to—come here, let's say. While we are ignorant is the time when this develops, and it grows and grows and grows; then, when it is explained what an addiction is, we already have it.

Dr. Hora: So you can get healed by reevaluating the experience. The issue is not that the cat loves us, but that we enjoy the idea that the cat loves us, and it makes us feel good to be so popular with the cat population (*laughing*).

Student: But then you feel bad about feeling good.

Dr. Hora: OK, then: Metapsychiatry says feelings do not indicate anything of validity. We are not here to feel good or to feel bad. It has nothing to do with love. Love is nonconditional benevolence. It is not a feeling. Being a cat lover is just self-love. The cat makes you feel good—jumps into your lap, jumps on your head, purrs. Some cats are very seductive, and there are many things in life that seem to make us feel good, and if something or someone makes us feel good, it is a warning sign.

Student: What is the spiritual counterpart?

Dr. Hora: As I said, perfect love is nonpersonal, nonconditional benevolence. You look at the cat with goodwill—as Schweitzer said, "reverence for life." Schweitzer wouldn't even step on an ant. He had reverence for all life forms, be they snakes or dogs or wild animals. We can appreciate the beauty of God's creation, and we have to respect it, and then we don't get attached.

Student: Dr. Hora, before you said if something makes us feel good, it is a warning sign. So what is the next step? Do we stop?

Dr. Hora: Be cruel? (*Laughter*) You have to see things in the context of God rather than interaction.

Student: So we can ask ourselves the meaning of this seeming experience of the cat making us feel good and understand what you said about how the fact that the cat loves us can be self-confirmatory. So we could ask the meaning, be honest with ourselves about what is really making us feel good in this situation.

Dr. Hora: Yes; if you understand the process of attachment, bonding, then you are alert: "That is not what the cat is here for. That is not what I am here for." We are here to see, understand, and acknowledge God's perfect universe. That everything and everyone is here for God…and there is great, glorious freedom and joy in being able to see life that way. It is the enlightened way. The enlightened way is perfect love. The definition of perfect love is worth repeating. It is nonpersonal, nonconditional benevolence. You see a tiger; it is beautiful. You don't have to embrace a tiger or get involved in interaction with a tiger.

Student: The meaning of this incessant need to bond and to become addicted—is it because people are specifically looking for love that this seems to be such a common occurrence? Everybody seems empty, and they want to fill something up?

Dr. Hora: All human beings are longing to be confirmed. That we're beautiful and good and worthwhile and special—and if nobody confirms it, then we do it ourselves. We look in the mirror and say, "You look gorgeous" (*laughing*).

The Zen masters are forever warning against becoming attached to one another or to anything in life. "Non-attachment" is their slogan for freedom and enlightened living, and perfect love makes it possible. No other love is really love except non-conditional benevolence. That is real love. Everything else is just trading: "I give you this and you give me that, and we give to each other." That is trading.

9

Walking Over a Broken Bridge Into the Village of the New Moon

―― ――

Student: I saw a television program last night called *Prophecy,* and it was prophesying some doom and gloom. Then it referred to a fellow named Cayce who could diagnose and cure illnesses from a distance. I am clear that it is not spiritual, but I don't know what it is. I would like to know, because many have confused it with being a spiritual idea, but it is all material. What is this special power some people have to see at a distance, diagnose illnesses, and know people's affairs when they have no contact with them?

Dr. Hora: Well, I don't know any details of this, but the public is very hungry for miracles—not divine miracles, but human miracles. Everybody would like to see some person who can perform miracles, because Jesus looked like he was a person who could perform miracles. But he said, "I can of mine own self do nothing," and that is the difference. Now, Edgar Cayce—I don't know the whole mythology about that guy Cayce. In order to know and to help people, he had to go to sleep (*laughing*). It's not Cayce; it's the people around him who wanted to see the miracles. There are always, everywhere in the world, all kinds of miracle makers. Indian gurus and everybody want to make miracles and see miracles performed by persons. Now, the moment there is a person, this is not spiritual.

But then, how many people are ready to understand that a non-person can be a medium through whom God manifests Himself as a healing, harmonizing power? So whenever somebody is performing personal miracles, chuck it. It's another hoax from another world. You don't have to worry about Edgar Cayce, because no person can perform any miracles. Hitler performed a great miracle. He murdered 6 million people. There are all kinds of miracles—miraculously powerful people—but it's not the individual; it's the human world that is anxiously seeking the power of God in the form of man. They speak of spirit. They speak of God. There are all kinds of things. There are churches—for instance, the Church of Religious Science, which is an offspring of Christian Science. But Christian Science never claimed that Mary Baker Eddy could heal people, or that her mind had the power to heal anybody. There are Religious Science churches all over the country, and they speak of the power of personal mind. They cultivate the belief that by studying these things, you can discover that your mind is better than someone else's mind, whereas the fact is, nobody has a mind of his own (*laughing*). Jesus never said, "I am smarter than anybody else, and my mind has this power to resurrect people and to heal people and to perform miracles." He didn't claim that, and that's the real problem. The moment somebody personalizes the power of God, he is a fake. It is a very interesting world, full of all kinds of things.

A Course in Miracles—someone wrote a book and gave it the title *A Course in Miracles*, which means that the human person can take a seminar, or listen to a series of lectures, or go to a place where they can teach him, to become a miracle worker as a person. When you believe something, you can give the impression that you personally went to a school where you have learned by taking a course to become a healer—a person who has the power to heal, which is not true. Nobody has the power to heal. Everybody can learn to know himself as a transparency for God. That means that if you are a beneficial presence in the world, the spirit of God is working through you, but you do not take credit for it. The moment you take personal credit for it, you are lost. That's the most difficult thing. The Zen master said, "Erase yourself utterly." What could he have meant? If you have erased yourself utterly, then you cannot take credit for anything.

Student: Can you hope for healing, though—that God will heal you? Right?

Dr. Hora: Yes. The problem is with hope. Hope is a problem. The idea of hope puts God in a time frame that doesn't exist. It is a future time frame—there is no such thing. There is no future, and there is no past. There is only now. Recently we were talking about a koan. How did it go?

Student: "Walking over a broken bridge."

Dr. Hora: Yes. "Walking over a broken bridge into the Village of the New Moon" (*laughing*). A well-known Zen koan. Who can understand it? If you don't understand it, you are not enlightened, and if you understand it, you are just walking in the right direction. (*Laughter*)

Student: The question is, how do you get to the Village of the New Moon if the bridge is broken?

Dr. Hora: Right.

Student: Is the word "over" significant?

Dr. Hora: No. They worry about how to get to the village, but on the other hand, you could ask, "What is this village?"

Student: I was considering this koan that you presented to me last week, and I saw the village as the beginning of a new life.

Dr. Hora: Yes. Exactly. So it is not a geographic location. Neither is it a community of neighbors, people, dogs, and such things.

Student: I also like the idea of the broken bridge meaning that once you get to the village, you can't go back to your old life. Once we have crossed over—once we understand what it means to cross over to the village—we can't go back. The bridge is broken. The past life is gone.

Dr. Hora: Yes. The past life never really was, and the new village is the new outlook on life. The moon is the permanent place of that village.

Student: We have to transcend this life.

Dr. Hora: Yes. Now, many religious thinkers speak of hope, and "hope" has become a respectable word in religious thinking— "hope." People don't stop to say, "Well, if I have to hope, then I have to hope for something that isn't yet." It is not *yet.* Whenever you hope for something, then you say there is something that is going to be but isn't yet. It doesn't make any sense for us to hope for anything. So many millions of people pray that their hopes would come true, and if we pray, hoping, then it will never be. How can God give us what we hope for? God cannot give us what we hope for. He can give us what already is. Take no thought for what should be or what should not be in the future; seek ye first to know the good of God, which already is. From moment to moment, it *is.* It is not something that hopefully will be. It's mind-boggling, isn't it?

Student: In the meantime, one doesn't hope. But if God has no time frame while we are under the illusion that we do have one, we think subconsciously, *I have to work this out.* We might even set ourselves a time period of a couple of days. This is a paradox, but it's also good. It gets complicated. We could say, "I am not at a level where I can solve this instantaneously," so we set up a time

period. How do we work with this knowing we are not fully realized, and that we seem to need time, yet not set up time as a barrier?
Hope.

Dr. Hora: We study Zen and Metapsychiatry in the hope that we will
eventually get it. (*Laughter*) But we don't have to hope that we
will get it. We just face the fact that it *is,* but we cannot see it. And
through meditation and mindfulness, facing the fact that for us it
is a problem now because we don't know what *is*. It is not something that *will be*. This can bring it to light, and sometimes we see.
I have known this koan at least 25 years, maybe more. It was so
obscure that I never even tried to understand it. I was fascinated,
yes, but I couldn't conceive that I could possibly understand. And
then one day, out of the blue, a thought comes that says, "If any
man is in Christ, he is a new creature: old things are passed away,
and behold, all things are become new" (2 Corinthians 5:17). This
is a Biblical statement. It comes to mind out of the blue that "if
any man is in Christ"—what does that mean? It means that if he
is imbued with the spirit of Christ, then he sees life in these terms:
the past never was, and everything is new. The Village of the New
Moon and the broken bridge. The broken bridge is gone, and everything is become new—this thought from the Bible suddenly
illuminated the meaning quite without my trying. It just burst forth
like a piece of light. This koan—this Japanese Zen koan—suddenly became clear, and before that, for 25 years, it was
incomprehensible. Even now, I hesitate. Sometimes I have to
search to see the connection between these things.

Student: What does the broken bridge represent?

Dr. Hora: The past is broken. Our approach to life is impassable because it is impossible; if our thoughts are stuck in temporality, in
time frames, then we cannot become enlightened. This is because
in enlightened consciousness there is no time and no space, and
there is nothing you can do or not do. The whole natural tendency

in us is to ask, "When was it?" "When will it be?" "How do you do it?" As long as this is our framework of thinking about life, we will never know the koan. The koan says there is no time, there is no space, there is no permanency, there is no impermanency; there is only the new moon, which means the moon is not a symbol of time. Even though they measure the months by the moon, all they can say about the moon is that it seems to be. All speculations about how long it will take or where it is—this is an entirely different way of perceiving life. Now, of course, if we know that there is no time and there is no space and there is nothing we can do, then we are enlightened. Stop wracking our brains about the problems of life, and we can be relaxed in the Reality of infinite good and immortality. Suddenly we are not afraid anymore to die, because we have died already to the world, which seems natural to all of us. So if we know the past never was, and there is no hope for us in the future, and there is nothing we can do either now or tomorrow, suddenly we understand immortality. And if we understand immortality, what is there to worry about? (*Laughing*)

Student: The only thing you have to worry about is being distracted, constantly distracted.

Dr. Hora: Not if you have understood the unreality of time and space and personal power. I have a little booklet about the teachings of Chuang-Tzu, a Chinese sage, and I lent it to one of my students. It is a beautiful little book, and she read it with great interest. That night, she had a nightmare from which she was jolted out of sleep. What was the nightmare? The nightmare was that she was on the open sea in a boat alone, and the boat was moving by itself. She had no paddles, nor any way of controlling the movement of the boat, and there she was all alone in the wide open sea with no way of controlling its movements. This frightened her tremendously so that she woke up. Now, who can understand this nightmare?

Student: God is in control.

Dr. Hora: She didn't dream about God.

Student: I suspect maybe her mode of being-in-the-world was altered, and it was scaring her.

Dr. Hora: Right. Exactly. Sure. She was in danger of becoming enlightened. No wonder we are afraid of these teachings (*laughing*).

Some years ago, I had a nightmare. It was a long time ago. I think at that time I was in Spain and I dreamed I was in a foreign city, I didn't know the language, I didn't know the city. I didn't know where to go and I didn't know anybody in that city, and I was completely lost with no communication possibilities with anybody around me. I didn't know where to go for what purpose or how to go. It was a big city, and I was in unfamiliar territory. That year I was in Barcelona, and I presented a paper there, and I also mentioned this nightmare, which I had at that same time. It was a very unpleasant thing, and it stayed with me for a while. Then, slowly, I remembered further parts of this dream—that I was desperate, not knowing where to turn and how to communicate and what to say, where to go—completely solitary. Then, suddenly, in the same dream, I found myself in a cathedral praying, all by myself. I saw a drop of rain falling down from the sky, and this raindrop hit the sun rays, and all the colors of the rainbow were suddenly illuminated in that raindrop. A great sense of peace descended, and then I woke up.

Made in the USA
Middletown, DE
22 December 2015